A Treasury of
Christmas
Miracles

A Treasury of Christmas Miracles

True Stories of God's Presence Today

Karen Kingsbury

New York   Boston   Nashville

Published in association with the literary agency of Alive Communications,
Inc., 7680 Goddard Street #200, Colorado Springs, CO 80920.

FaithWords
Hachette Book Group
237 Park Avenue
New York, NY 10017

www.faithwords.com

Printed in the United States of America

First Edition: October 2001
Reissued: September 2007
10   9   8   7

FaithWords is a division of Hachette Book Group, Inc.
The FaithWords name and logo is a trademark of Hachette Book Group, Inc.

Library of Congress Cataloging-in-Publication Data

Kingsbury, Karen
   A treasury of Christmas miracles : true stories of God's presence today /
   Karen Kingsbury
      p. cm.
   ISBN 0-446-52959-1
   1. Miracles. 2. Christmas--Miscellanea. I Title.
   BT97.3 .K56 2001
   242'.335--dc21   2001026331

Interior design: Charles Sutherland

LCCN: 2007928517
ISBN 978-0-446-19392-4

To my amazing husband and wonderful children,
Kelsey, Tyler, Austin, Sean, Joshua, and EJ.
And to God Almighty,
who has, for now, blessed me with these,
the greatest gifts of all.

Preface

I love Christmas—everything about it.

December arrives with its strains of "Joy to the World" and all its traditions: carolers and twinkling lights, shopping sales, ribbons of red and green, and festive packages placed carefully under the tree.

Christmas is also a time to mark our progress through this earthly journey. Every December we can look back and marvel at the designs of God and realize how very little we are in control of the events that shaped the past year. Then, with hearts full, look to the celebration of that silent, holy night, and all its certainty. Because of Christmas, this we know: Christ was born for us. He is love, and the plans he has for us always surpass those of our own.

I understand that better with each passing year.

Last season my sister and I hit the malls the day after Thanksgiving and were part of a throng of shoppers hunting bargains long before the sun came up. In the process I was struck, as I am each year, by the way in which we hustle through the season. Searching for bargains, desperate for the right gift at the right price, and often so busy we barely notice the tinny refrains of

"Silent Night" announcing over the store's P.A. system that all is calm, all is bright.

Unfortunately, we live with a sense of urgency for all the wrong reasons. Perhaps our time would be better spent looking for the miracles that so clearly exist around us. Especially during the Christmas season. Miracles remind us that God loves us and that on that first Christmas so long ago he gave us the best present of all. His love continues day by day—often through his miracles.

For this reason I bring you a collection of Christmas miracles. Though the stories are true, they have been fictionalized to protect the privacy of the people involved.

All of us are in need of a miracle. Thankfully, such stories abound if only we will have eyes to see them—to look for them. I hope the accounts here will help make this holiday more meaningful for you and yours. Perhaps they will give you a reason to reach out to someone in need. Or maybe they will provide you with comfort as you grieve over the recent loss of a loved one.

Now more than ever I am struck by the contrast of our own busy Christmas preparations compared to the lack of attention it received two thousand years ago. On the night of the actual event, not a single innkeeper had room to house the King of kings. They missed the greatest miracle of all!

Look around your life this Christmas. Watch for the miracles of the season.

I pray that those of us who prepare so well for the holiday celebration might not miss the reason for it. Regardless of how full our lives are, I hope we still have room in our hearts to look for the one whose birth forever changed the world. The one who is—indeed—still working Christmas miracles among us.

I still love hearing from you. Please visit my Web site at www.KarenKingsbury.com. You can connect with other readers, view my ongoing journal and photos of my family, and pray for the military men and women posted on my site. You can also leave a comment or a question, and submit military photos so that people all over the world can pray for your loved one serving our country.

I pray you and yours will find time to marvel at the manger this Christmas, and that in doing so you will experience the greatest gift of all.

Until next time . . . in His light and love,

Karen Kingsbury

That Silent Night

*I*t was exactly one month before Christmas when Katy Anderson got word that her mother was dying of cancer in their hometown an hour out of Des Moines, Iowa. At just twenty-one years old, Katy was newly married and living several states away when she received the tragic news.

Her mother was only forty-five and, worse yet, she was alone and unable to care for herself.

"I can't let Mom die by herself." Tears streamed down Katy's face as her husband, Steve, held her close. "She was always there for me; now it's time for me to be there for her."

Although the couple's first Christmas together

was fast approaching, they dipped into their savings ac-
count and scraped together enough money for Katy to fly
to Iowa. It was a one-way ticket.

"God will help us find a way to be together, Katy."
Steve kissed her good-bye at the airport, unashamed of the
tears in his eyes. "Christmas is about miracles, after all."

Time passed and though Katy's mother greatly ap-
preciated her presence, Katy was secretly terrified. Not
only would she have to be strong while her mother
wasted away, but she would have to do so without the
love and support of Steve.

"You miss him, don't you?" Katy's mother took her
hand one afternoon. "Go home, sweetheart. I'll be fine.
Me and the Lord had a little talk and he's expecting me
any time."

2

Katy shook her head and smiled, ignoring the heavi-
ness that welled up in her heart. "I won't leave you alone.
Besides, Steve says Christmas is a time for miracles. God
will find some way for us to all be together."

Back home in Montana, Steve stood up in church the
Sunday before Christmas and asked the congregation to
pray for him. "I want to be with Katy and her mother."
He paused, meeting the eyes of friends and family he'd
known for years at First Central Community Church.
"Pray that God will work a miracle and find me a way
there."

It was nearly a three-day drive from Billings, Montana, to Katy's mother's house in Iowa, and though Steve's
boss had agreed to give him five days off around Christmas, there was no way he could make the round-trip by

car and still have time with Katy and her mother. Finally, three days before Christmas Steve got a call.

"Heard you need a little answer to prayer." It was Joe Isaacson, a local business executive and longtime First Central church member. Joe owned a two-seater Cessna that he often took out on the weekends as a way of relaxing. He was planning to fly on Wednesday, December 23, and was willing to go quite a ways farther if Steve needed a ride to Iowa.

Especially at Christmastime.

Chills made their way along Steve's arms and legs. He thanked Joe and made plans for when to meet him; then he called Katy and told her the news. "We're going to be together after all, honey. I knew God would give us a Christmas miracle if we asked him."

Katy was quiet on the other end. "Hurry, Steve. Mom . . . she isn't doing well."

Small planes were not high on Steve Anderson's list of reliable modes of transportation, let alone means of relaxation. In fact, he'd never flown before and had always figured when the time came to board a plane it would be a jumbo jet. But the opportunity to fly from Montana to Iowa to see his wife for Christmas was too irresistible for Steve to pass up.

"It's a small plane, but smooth as silk in the air," Joe told him the day before the flight. "Tell you what—you can be my navigator."

In the recesses of his mind, Steve felt a slight wave of anxiety course through his body. He swallowed his fears and cleared his throat.

"I've never done any navigating," he said with a laugh. "But I'd be willing to fly the plane myself if it meant getting back to my wife at Christmas."

Steve met Joe the next day at a small airport outside of town. The morning was beautiful, clear and without any trace of bad weather. Strains of "Silent Night" played on the airport loudspeaker.

"The weather's beautiful. Looks like we picked a good day to hit the skies," Joe said, easily shifting his body into the cockpit.

Steve sized up the tiny aircraft and silently, almost unconsciously, whispered a prayer: *Lord, guide us as we go, and please get us there safely.*

For the first hour the craft flew easily through the clear skies, but as they neared the halfway point of their flight they entered a thick fog.

"No problem," Joe said, pointing out the windshield. "You can see radio towers there above the fog. If we keep our eyes on them we'll know where we are. Besides, we have aviation maps on board. Everything will be fine."

For a while, it looked as if Joe would be right. Then, when the plane was just outside Pierre, South Dakota, the fog worsened so that the plane became cocooned in a cloud with no visibility whatsoever.

Almost at the same time, the plane's radio and instruments died. Suddenly the men could no longer see anything on the ground, and because of the instrument failure they couldn't monitor the fuel or talk to people in the control tower.

Steve may have been inexperienced at flying, but he

did not need a pilot's license to know they were in grave danger. His thoughts turned to his wife and he began begging God for survival. *Please, God, help us,* he prayed silently, his hands clenched and his face white with terror. *Please, get us through this safely.*

At that moment they flew through a clearing in the fog and caught a glimpse of Pierre Municipal Airport just below. Joe maneuvered the craft through the opening in the clouds and smoothly down onto the runway.

"Thank God," Steve whispered as the men climbed out of the plane and Joe began tinkering with the fuse box. A burned-out fuse had caused the instrument failure, and Joe replaced it while Steve telephoned Katy.

"Listen, honey," Steve told Katy, "we're running late because of bad weather. Meet me at the airport about an hour later than we planned."

"Is everything okay? With the plane, I mean?" she asked. Steve could hear how Katy was trying to control the concern in her voice.

"It's fine," he said, sounding more confident than he felt. "And guess what? My boss says I can stay through New Year's. It's going to be the best Christmas ever, just being there with you and your mom. I love you, honey. See you in a few hours."

As they climbed back in the craft, Steve again uttered a silent prayer: *you got us this far, God. Please see us through safely to Iowa.*

In less than an hour, the men were back in the sky, enjoying the fact that the sun had come out and the conditions were once again clear. By the time they flew over

Sioux Falls, Steve's fears had nearly disappeared and he began looking forward to being with Katy.

Then, as the plane passed over a series of valleys, the fog appeared once more and almost instantly engulfed the small craft in a dense, suffocating blanket of gray. Moments later they approached a mountain range, and Steve watched as Joe struggled to clear it safely.

"After these mountains, it should be sunny again," Joe said, struggling to convince himself as much as Steve. "There's never fog in this area."

But as night fell there was indeed fog, and it was so thick the men could see nothing past the plane's windshield. The airport wasn't far away, and Joe immediately contacted the radio control tower for assistance.

"We're closed because of fog," the air traffic controller informed Joe. "We have no capability for instrument landing. Return to Pierre Municipal Airport and land there."

"That's more than an hour back; I can't," Joe said, a tinge of panic creeping into his voice. "We're almost out of fuel. We don't have enough to fly back to Pierre."

For a moment, the cockpit was eerily silent. They had no visibility, and Steve's eyes fell on the fuel gauge and the needle, which danced dangerously over the letter E. Again he silently prayed, struggling to control his terror: *please, God, please get us out of these clouds safely. Let me make it home this Christmas, please . . .*

Finally, a different voice broke the silence. "Okay. We'll get the ground crew ready. Come in on an emergency landing."

That Silent Night

Steve clutched the side of his seat, his eyes wide in disbelief. There was no way they could make an emergency landing when visibility between the plane and the control tower was completely cut off by the fog.

Joe's voice snapped Steve to attention.

"Get the aviation maps."

Steve opened them instantly, and Joe estimated their location. According to the map, they should be directly above the airport. Gradually, Joe began to descend through the fog toward the ground. As he did, the voice of the controller entered the cockpit.

"Pull it up! Pull it up!"

Joe responded immediately, just as both men saw a split in the fog. They were not over the airport as they had thought. Instead they were over the lights of a busy interstate highway and had missed an overpass by no more than five feet.

Steve felt his heart thumping wildly, and he was struck by the certainty of one thing. Short of divine intervention, there was no way they would escape their grave situation alive. The memory of "Silent Night" playing in the airport earlier that day rewound itself in Steve's mind. Now the words took on a terrifyingly different meaning. Without anyone to guide them down from the skies, the silence in their cockpit that night might be the last they would ever know.

At that instant, the controller's voice broke the silence again. "If you will listen to me, I'll help you get down," he said.

Joe released a pent-up sigh. "Go ahead. I'm listening."

Steve closed his eyes momentarily and prayed, begging God to guide them safely through the fog onto the ground.

Meanwhile, the controller began guiding Joe toward a landing.

"Come down a little. Okay, a little more. Not that much. All right, now over to the right. Straighten it out and come down a little more."

The calm, reassuring voice of the controller continued its steady stream of directions, and Joe, intent on the voice, did as he was instructed. The trip seemed to take an eternity, and Steve wondered whether he would see his wife again. "Please, God," he whispered. "Get us onto the ground. Please."

The controller continued. "Raise it a little more. Okay, you're too far to the left. That's right. Now lower it a little more. All right, you're right over the end of the runway. Set it down. Now!"

Carefully responding just as he was told, Joe lowered the plane, and when he was a few feet from the ground the runway came into sight. As the plane touched down, Steve saw Katy standing nearby waiting for him, and his eyes filled with tears of relief and gratitude.

The two men in the cockpit looked at each other. Without saying a word, they bowed their heads and closed their eyes. "Thank you, God," Steve said, his voice choked with emotion. "Thank you for sparing our lives today. And thank you for listening."

Joe picked up the plane's radio and contacted the control tower. "Hey, I just want to thank you for what you did. We couldn't have made it without those directions. You probably saved our lives."

There was a brief pause. "What are you talking about?" the controller asked. He had a different voice this time, and he was clearly confused. "We lost all radio contact with you when we told you to return to Pierre."

Goose bumps rose up on Steve's arms and he watched as Joe's face went blank in disbelief. "You what?" he asked.

"We never heard from you again, and we never heard you talking to us or to anyone else," the controller said. "We were stunned when we saw you break through the clouds right over the runway. It was a perfect landing."

Steve and Joe looked at each other in silent amazement. If this controller hadn't been in contact with them through the emergency landing, who had? Whose calm, clear voice had filled the cockpit with the directions that saved their lives?

Today Steve is aware that he still cannot specifically answer those questions. But in his heart he is certain that God did indeed grant him a Christmas miracle that December night.

"I believe that God protected us that day and that perhaps he allowed an angel to guide us to the ground safely," Steve says. "It was a Christmas when Katy and I desperately needed to be together. God sustained me through that silent night and he continues to do so every day of my life."

A Helping Hand

*A*dam Armstrong received the call just after nine on Christmas Day while on patrol with the sheriff's department in Akron, Ohio. A woman was weeping loudly in a corner booth at a truck stop on the highway outside of town. Several patrons had grown concerned and contacted the sheriff's department.

Armstrong sighed and turned his patrol car in the direction of the truck stop. As a veteran officer of eight years, he had seen so much pain in the lives of people that he could only imagine what might cause a woman to weep aloud in a truck stop.

Especially on Christmas Day.

As he drove the remaining three miles, he remembered how the pain people suffered had been the reason he had joined the police force in the first place. He had ridden along with a police officer one night as part of the research for a local newspaper story he was writing. The first call of the night involved a woman who had been badly beaten by her husband. Armstrong watched as the officer handcuffed the man and led him away; he saw the relief on the woman's face, and suddenly something clicked. He might write a thousand stories about good and evil in the course of a lifetime. But none of them could do for that woman what the police officer had just done. No story could ever rescue her from her pain.

Armstrong sought police work the very next day and never once looked back. Now, eight years later, his love for his work was as strong as it had been in the beginning. Despite the danger and frustration that came with the job, there were always nights like that one in which he could still make a difference for someone in pain.

Not sure what he would find, Armstrong entered the truck stop café—aglow with Christmas lights—and immediately spotted the woman, still weeping, her face covered with her hands. Nearby sat two frightened little blonde girls who seemed to be around four and five years old.

Armstrong's face softened as he approached the children.

"What seems to be the matter, girls?" he asked them. The older child turned to look at him, and Armstrong could see she had tears in her eyes, too.

11

"Daddy couldn't get us no Christmas presents, so he left us," she said. "He put our stuff out of the car while we was in the bathroom."

Armstrong's heart sank. He studied the woman and gently placed a hand on her shoulder. Then he looked at the girls and smiled a warm, comforting smile. "Well, now, is that so?"

The children nodded.

"In that case I want you two to climb on those stools over there and order something to eat."

Reluctantly the girls walked away from their mother and took separate stools along the counter. Armstrong signaled the waitress and asked her to get the girls whatever they wanted from the menu.

12

With the children out of earshot, the officer sat down across from the woman. She looked up from her hands and stared sadly at Armstrong, her eyes filled with heartbreak.

"What's the problem?" Armstrong asked quietly.

"It's what my girl said," the woman replied, wiping her eyes. "My husband's not cruel. Just at the end of his rope. We're flat broke, and he figured we'd get more help alone than if he stayed. I've been sitting here praying about what to do next, but I don't even have the money for a phone call. It hasn't been a very good Christmas, sir." Fresh tears appeared. "But right now I just want to know God is listening, you know?"

Armstrong nodded, his eyes gentle and empathetic. And silently he added his own prayer, asking God to show him a way to help this woman and her little children. Armstrong believed with all his heart that God had used angels to protect him in the line of duty on more than one occasion, and he had faith he could do the same for this family.

She needs an angel about now, Lord, he prayed silently. *Please help her out.*

Armstrong broke the silence between them. "Do you have family?"

"The nearest is in Tulsa."

Armstrong thought a moment, then suggested several agencies that could help her. As they spoke, the waitress brought hot dogs and French fries to the children, so the officer stood up and moved toward the counter. He took out his wallet to pay the bill. *It'll be my Christmas present to her,* he thought.

13

"The boss says no charge," the waitress said. "We know what's going on here."

Armstrong smiled at the woman and nodded his thanks. Then he stooped to ask the girls how they liked their food. As he did, a trucker stood up from his table and approached the waitress. He mumbled something to her, and then she took him by the arm and led him to Armstrong.

It was unusual for a truck driver to approach Armstrong on his own. Typically truck drivers and police officers had something of a natural animosity for each other. Most truck drivers tended to see the police as cutting into their earnings by writing them tickets, while the police saw truckers as reckless people who placed their potential earnings before safety. The truth, of course, was somewhere in the middle. But still, Armstrong couldn't remember a time when he'd been approached by a truck driver outside of the line of duty.

The trucker wore jeans, a T-shirt, and a baseball cap. He walked up to the counter and stood alongside Armstrong. The officer noticed that the normal buzz of conversation and activity had stilled and the café was silent. Most of the patrons—nearly all of them long-distance truckers—were watching the conversation between the trucker and the officer.

"Excuse me, Officer," the man said. "Here."

The trucker reached out his hand and gave the officer a fistful of bills. He cleared his throat.

"We passed the hat. There ought to be enough to get the woman and her girls started on their way."

14

Back when he was a boy, Armstrong had learned that cops don't cry, at least not in public. So he stood there, speechless until the lump in his throat disappeared and he was able to speak.

Then Armstrong shook the man's hand firmly. "I'm sure she'll appreciate it," he said, his voice gruff from covering up his emotion. "Can I tell her your name?"

The trucker raised his hands and backed away from the officer. "Nope. Just tell her it was from folks with families of their own. Folks who wish they were home for Christmas, too."

Armstrong nodded and thought of the fiercely loyal way in which people who made their living on the road looked out for each other. As the trucker walked away, Armstrong counted the money and was again amazed. A small room of truck drivers had in a matter of minutes raised two hundred dollars, enough money for three bus tickets to Tulsa and food along the way.

The officer walked back to the booth and handed the money to the woman, at which point she began to sob again.

"He heard," she whispered through her tears.

"Ma'am?" Armstrong was confused, wondering who the woman was talking about.

"Don't you see?" she said. "I came here completely desperate, hopeless. And I sat in this booth and asked God to help us, to give us a sign that he still loved us and cared for us."

Armstrong felt chills along his arms and remembered his own prayer—how he had asked God to send help and provide this woman with angelic assistance. The truck drivers certainly didn't look like a textbook group of angels, but God had used them all the same. "You know, ma'am, I think you're right. I think he really did hear."

At that instant, a young couple entered the truck stop, saw the sobbing woman, and approached her without hesitating. They introduced themselves and asked if they could help in any way.

"Well," the woman said, "I could use a ride to the bus stop. See, I've got the money now, and I need to get to . . ."

Armstrong stood up and walked discreetly away from the scene to a quiet corner of the truck stop, where he radioed dispatch.

"The situation's resolved," he said.

Then he walked toward his patrol car and climbed inside. Not until he was safely out of sight did he let the tears come—tears that assured him he would never forget what had happened that night in the truck stop. As a patrol officer, he almost always saw the worst in people around him. But that night, he'd been reminded that kindness and love do exist among men. And Armstrong had learned something else. Sometimes God answered prayer using nothing more than a dozen bighearted truckers sharing coffee at a truck stop outside of Akron, Ohio—and playing the part of Christmas angels.

The Most Wonderful Time of the Year

*P*aul Jacobs was working in the yard of his home in Austin, Texas, thinking about his brother, Vince. It was Christmastime, the most wonderful time of the year, yet Vince lay in the hospital struggling with a serious bout of appendicitis. *Help him, God . . . It's Christmas . . . Let him come home, Lord. Please . . .* He'd barely finished uttering the silent prayer when his wife, Laura, yelled to say he'd received a call from his brother's wife. He walked into the house, wiped the sweat from his brow, and picked the receiver up off the countertop.

"Paul, you'd better get down here quickly," Vince's wife blurted out. Paul could tell she was distraught.

"Vince?"

"Yes." She began to cry, and Paul's heart went out to her. "The infection's all through his body. Doctors say it doesn't look good. Please, Paul, hurry."

Paul hung up the phone and moved toward his wife, who had joined him from the next room when she realized the call was about Vince.

"I can't believe it," Paul said. "That was Ruth. She said Vince is worse. The doctors think we should all be there."

"You mean he might not make it?" Laura was astonished.

"I guess not. We better get down there and see what's happening."

Paul grabbed his car keys, stunned at the turn of events. His brother, Vince, was only thirty-seven and had been healthy and strong until the previous week, when he'd been hospitalized with appendicitis. Doctors had removed the appendix, but during the procedure the organ had burst, spewing poisonous infection throughout his body.

At first antibiotics seemed to handle the invasion of infection throughout his system. But the day before, Vince's fever had begun to rise and the family had again grown concerned. Still, even the doctors hadn't thought Vince's illness could be life threatening until now.

Paul thought about what would happen if his older brother died and shuddered. Vince was in the prime of his life, and he and Ruth had two young children.

Silently Paul prayed that God would spare him and give his body strength to fight the infection.

Paul and Laura drove the five miles to the hospital, where they met up with Paul's parents.

"Is it really as bad as Ruth said?" Paul searched his father's eyes for an answer.

"It's serious, son. Very serious. We need to pray."

The sudden change in Vince's condition had caught his father by surprise also. Sam Jacobs and his oldest son worked together in a family-run farm-equipment business. He saw Vince nearly every day and knew him to be strong and in good health.

"If anyone can pull through this thing, Vince will," the older man continued. "But let's pray all the same."

Paul nodded and turned to hug his mother, Ronni. He saw that she had tears in her eyes, and he squeezed her hands in his.

"He's going to be all right, Mom," Paul assured her. "God won't let anything happen to him. Not with those little kids waiting for him back at home."

Ronni nodded, but she knew that might not be true. Sometimes people died and there wasn't any earthly explanation for their death. Bad things happened in life. Even to praying people. Ronni believed there was a reason behind such occurrences, but usually that reason remained a mystery. And the knowledge of that never made the tragedy easier to accept.

"Let's ask God to be merciful," she suggested softly.

The foursome moved quietly down the sterile corridors of the hospital to the intensive-care waiting room.

For the next few hours there was little conversation as they passed the time praying and waiting for word from the doctors.

At about five o'clock that evening, the primary doctor responsible for treating Vince entered the room. By then Vince's sister and her family had joined the others, and the waiting room was full of people worried about Vince.

"I'm afraid I don't have very good news," the doctor said softly, tucking his hands into his white medical jacket. "Vince's fever is very, very high and the blood tests show he's no longer responding to the antibiotics."

In many ways the doctor's words came as no surprise, but still, Vince's family puzzled over what was happening.

"Doctor, these complications are all a result of my son's appendicitis?" Sam asked.

The doctor shook his head pensively and pursed his lips. "No, not exactly. The appendix became inflamed and caused the initial problem. Then, when it burst during surgery, the infection inside spread through Vince's bloodstream, sending his entire system into immediate trauma."

He paused a moment, searching for the easiest terms with which to explain the situation. "Because of that, he's now fighting against peritonitis and infection throughout his body. When that happens, the situation is very serious, and the outcome depends on how easily the person's immune system can handle the invading infection.

"In Vince's case, his body attempted to fight the problem, and then for some reason it shut down. At this point the infection is out of control, and there's nothing else we can do for him except continue to administer massive antibiotics."

"Doctor, when you say 'nothing else we can do for him,' does that mean he might die?" Ronni sounded brave as she asked the question, but the others knew she was on the verge of breaking down.

"Yes, I'm afraid so. If something doesn't change, I don't think he'll make it through the night."

Laura muffled a gasp, while Ruth hung her head and sighed. Sam cleared his throat, his chin quivering with emotion. "When can we see him, sir?"

"Immediate family may take turns now. Just one at a time, though," the doctor said. Then he paused uncomfortably. This part of his job never got easier. "I'm sorry about all of this. Let's hope for a miracle."

21

Then he turned and left the Jacobs family alone to deal with the blow. Ruth stood up, tears flooding her eyes, and headed toward the door.

"I'll go see him first," she said. "I'll tell him you're all here. Maybe it'll help."

Ruth was prepared for what she saw when she entered her husband's room, but it was still painfully difficult. Vince was hooked up to IV tubing and his body was red with the heat of his fever. His eyes were closed and he appeared to be caught up in a fitful sleep. Could this be the same man who had been the picture of health only a week ago?

"Honey, it's me," she whispered, leaning over his bed.

Vince moaned, and Ruth was fairly sure he couldn't understand her. His fever was so high he had become delirious. Ruth took his hand, cringing at how hot it felt in her own.

"Listen, now, Vince," she said, her voice cracking with emotion. "Everyone's here; they're out in the lobby. And they're praying for you, Vince. We all want you to hurry up and fight this thing so you can come home for Christmas. You hear me, honey?"

There was no response, and a single sob escaped from Ruth's throat.

"Vince, please don't die. We need you. Hang in there, sweetheart." She ran her fingers tenderly over his blazing hot forehead as her tears fell on his hospital bed. "I love you, Vince."

When Ruth returned, Sam took a turn, and then Ronni, and when they had both come back to the waiting room, Laura and Paul exchanged a glance.

"You go," Paul said. "I'll go next."

It was after eight in the evening by then and the hospital had grown quiet. Laura left the room and disappeared down the hallway. The others were quiet, lost in their own thoughts and sadness.

A few minutes passed, and then the silence in the room was interrupted as a heavyset, elderly woman leaned into the room. Immediately Sam and Ronni recognized her as one of their longtime neighbors, Sadie Johnson. She was in her late seventies, a devoutly faithful woman who spent most of her days volunteering at church. Despite the walker she needed to get around, she was healthy and still spent an hour each day working in her flower garden.

"Well, I'll be," she said cheerfully. "What are you good folks doing hanging around a hospital on a cold night like this?"

Sam nodded toward Sadie politely. "Evening, Sadie. I didn't know you were ill. You been in the hospital long?"

"Naaa," Sadie said. "Just here for a few routine tests. You know those doctors, poking and prodding and taking pictures just to tell you everything's fine." She glanced at the clock on the wall. "Well, it's about bedtime so I better get going. Just thought I'd take a stroll through the place and see if anything exciting was going on."

She looked at the many faces of the Jacobs family as they sat solemnly in the waiting room, and suddenly her face fell with concern.

"Sam, is everything okay? You people look mighty upset." Sam hung his head, afraid he might cry, and Ronni answered for him.

"It's our son Vince, the oldest. He has infection all through his body." She reached for her husband's hand. "The doctors told us he probably won't live through the night."

Sadie looked appalled. "Well, now that's just not right. Vince's a young thing, isn't he? Thirty-something? And at Christmastime? That's terrible."

"Thirty-seven," Ronni said softly. "His children are very young."

23

"Thirty-seven!" Sadie repeated, shaking her head. "And little kids, too." The older woman shifted positions, pulling her robe more closely around her body. "Well, I believe I'm going to have a talk tonight with the Man upstairs and ask him to let me go in Vince's place. I wanted to be home for Christmas, anyway." She grinned and her eyes sparkled. "You know." She pointed upward. "My real home. Up there with the Lord and my dear sweet honey-pie, Kenny." She nodded confidently. "That's just what I'll do—ask the Lord if I can leave here in place of Vince."

The Jacobs family looked at her in unison, startled by her statement. "Now, Sadie, that's not necessary," Sam said quickly. "We're praying for Vince and we'll pray for you, too, so that—"

Sadie waved a hand, interrupting Sam. "No, no. Don't go doing that. I don't need no one praying for me no more." She smiled peacefully. "Sam, I'm more than ready to go home. I've loved our dear Lord all my life, and I'm getting too tired to stay around here anymore. I want to go home soon and it might as well be tonight."

She thought a moment before continuing.

"Here's what I'm hoping to do. Tonight I'm going to ask God to be kind and generous with me. I'll ask him to take me in Vince's place so that come tomorrow morning Vince'll be on the road to recovery and I'll be on the road to the Pearly Gates. I'll spend Christmas in heaven and Vince can spend it with his family. Wouldn't that just be the best thing yet?"

Sam was silent a moment, unsure of how to react.

"Well, that's all settled," Sadie said, sounding very sure of herself. "Everything will be just fine for the both of us." She smiled at Sam and Ronni and then at the others.

"I'll get to see Kenny on the other side," she said, winking once. Then she shuffled away.

Laura returned from Vince's room just as Sadie was leaving. "Wasn't that your old neighbor?" she asked Sam and Ronni as she sat down.

Ronni nodded, still perplexed by Sadie's unusual words. "She said the strangest thing. She's going to pray that God takes her home tonight in Vince's place. She's tired of living, she's lived long enough, and she's ready to join God and her dead husband in heaven—just in time for Christmas."

Laura raised an eyebrow and looked at the others in the room. "She said that?"

"Now don't put truth into her words," one of them said in response. "God doesn't work like that, taking one life in place of another."

Sam had been very quiet, staring intently at his hands. Now he looked up and spoke. "You never know about God," he said. "He works in mysterious ways. Scripture says the prayer of a righteous person is powerful and effective. And I don't know many people as righteous—really righteous in the way God intended—as Sadie Johnson."

There was silence again and Paul privately pondered the woman's faith and her lack of fear regarding death. He didn't expect anything to come of her strange proclamation, but he felt Sadie's words revealed a great deal of wisdom. The thought of going to heaven was one of pure joy for Sadie Johnson, not sadness or sorrow. For people as close to God as she was, death was merely a journey to the other side. Paul felt filled with peace and decided that the woman had in some ways made facing Vince's impending death easier.

Before midnight, Paul and Laura and several of the others returned home for a few hours' sleep.

"We'll be back before sunup," Paul said, bending to kiss his mother on the cheek. "Call us if anything changes."

Ronni nodded. She and Sam intended to stretch out on the waiting room sofas. Vince was their son, after all. They wanted to be nearby if Ruth or Vince needed them for any reason.

26

Three hours passed as Sam and Ronni drifted in and out of sleep. Several times during the night they checked on Vince and Ruth, but Vince's condition remained critical. At six the next morning, Paul and Laura returned to the waiting room and nudged Paul's parents awake.

"How is he?" Paul asked.

"We haven't heard anything since a few hours ago," Sam said, sitting up and rubbing his eyes. "He must still be hanging in there."

Paul and Laura sat down and held hands, bracing themselves for whatever sorrow the day might hold. They stayed that way for the next hour as other family members arrived in ones and twos.

Then, just before eight o'clock, Vince's doctor burst through the door, a broad smile on his face.

"His fever broke," the doctor announced. "Sometime in the last couple of hours he began making a turn-around, and now his fever is almost down to normal. I have no way of explaining what happened—I've never seen anything like it before." He paused. "Merry Christmas!"

Tears of relief flooded the family's eyes. Sam rose from the couch and shook the doctor's hand. "Thank you, sir," he said. "Does that mean he's going to pull through this?"

"He's a new man today, Mr. Jacobs. I think he's going to be just fine."

The doctor left and the Jacobs family leaned back in their seats, thankful and relieved.

"Thank God," Ronni said. "Thank God for hearing our prayers."

At the mention of prayer, several of them remembered Sadie Johnson and sat straighter in their chairs. They exchanged glances.

"Dad," Paul said, his eyes wider than before, "you don't think this has something to do with what Mrs. Johnson said last night, do you?"

"Of course not," Sam scoffed. "God wasn't ready to take Vince home; that's all there is to it."

Paul nodded, but his curiosity got the better of him and he excused himself from the group.

"I'm taking a little walk," he explained. "Be right back."

Laura watched him go and knew where he was headed. She hoped Mrs. Johnson would be happy with the news of Vince's recovery.

Out in the corridor, Paul walked toward the front desk and asked what floor Sadie Johnson was on.

"She's on the third floor, sir," the receptionist said. "Room 325, in the observation unit."

Paul thanked the woman and rode the elevator to the third floor. There he approached the nurses' station and waited until someone noticed him.

"Can I help you, sir?" a woman asked. Paul glanced at the name on her badge and saw that she was the head nurse for that floor.

"Yes, ma'am, I'm looking for our neighbor, Mrs. Sadie Johnson. She's a friend of our family's. I understand she's in Room 325."

The nurse's eyes fell. "I'm sorry, sir," she said, unsure of whether she should tell him what happened. "Mrs. Johnson passed away a few hours ago."

Paul felt his heart skip a beat as he stood frozen in place, stunned by the news. "But I thought she was only in for routine tests."

"That's right, sir, she was." The nurse lowered her clipboard and frowned. "Then a few hours ago her heart just stopped. We worked with her for some time trying to bring her back, but her body didn't respond. I'm sorry."

Paul thanked the nurse and turned back down the hallway to the elevator. He felt as though he were in a trance as he walked through the hospital to the waiting room on the first floor. When he entered the room, the others saw how strange he looked and the room became quiet.

"What is it, Paul?" Sam asked, worried that Vince might have taken another sudden turn for the worse.

"It's Mrs. Johnson, Dad." Paul's voice was flat, void of emotion. "She's dead. She died a few hours ago—about the same time Vince began making a comeback."

"That's impossible," Ronni said. "Mrs. Johnson was only here for routine tests."

"The nurse told me her heart stopped," Paul added. "She went to sleep last night and died before she ever woke up."

The room grew silent again as each of them absorbed the amazing truth. Sadie Johnson had prayed for Vince to live, asking God to let her go in his place. Now that very thing had happened and doctors had no explanation for either Vince's recovery or Sadie's death.

"Do you think what happened was an answer to her prayer?" Paul asked, looking incredulously at the other faces in the room.

For a moment no one spoke. Then Sam sat up straighter and tilted his head thoughtfully.

"Well, son, I don't think there's one of us here who can discount the truth of what's happened these past few hours. Sure as I'm sitting here today, I'm convinced that Sadie returned to her room last night and asked God in all his mercy to take her home and let Vince live."

He looked at the others. "And sure enough, that's

what happened." A sad smile came across his face. "Now they'll both be home for Christmas.

"I guess it's like we were saying last night. The prayer of a righteous person is powerful and effective. Whatever we do, let's not forget that. Because that might just be all the explanation we'll ever get for what's just happened here."

Jessica's Gift

*N*estled in the heart of the town of Cottonwood, Arizona, behind the post office in an unassuming house lived a little girl named Jessica Warner. In many ways there was nothing unusual about Jessica. She was five years old with naturally curly, golden blonde hair and blue eyes that shone with unfettered joy. She had a smile that brightened any room even in a town where the sun shone almost every day of the year. And she had a favorite doll named Molly, tattered and smudged and loved into a raggedy state.

The Warner family loved everything about living in Cottonwood. It was a town where parents visited at weekend soccer games and people waved at each other up and down Main Street whether they knew you or not. Joe Anderson, the barber, and Steven Simmons, the paint store manager, hung signs in their windows stating, "Mingus Rocks" as a way of cheering on the Mingus High School football team, which every year toyed with the idea of a state title. It was a town where doors went unlocked, children played safely on their rock-garden front yards, and teens complained about having nothing to do.

Although the seasons didn't leave their mark on Cottonwood the way they might in a midwestern town or a seaport along the Atlantic Ocean, the Warners savored the subtle changes. Sparkling spring days, when the sun played on the distant red rocks of Sedona; the heat of summer, when great monsoons would sweep into the Verde Valley; and fall, when the wind kicked up and Yavapai County Fairgrounds played host to the annual Harvest Festival.

32

But really, the months were like a yearlong crescendo building their way to the Warners' favorite time of all: the Christmas season, when the high-desert town of Cottonwood came to life as miraculously—the townspeople suspected—as Bethlehem had some two thousand years earlier.

The official arrival of the Christmas season was marked each year with the ritual of the city manager and his deputy climbing up the ladder on Ernie Gray's fire truck and stringing the "Happy Holidays" garland across Main Street. Between then and the morning of the Christmas parade, homeowners around town took part in an unofficial house-decorating contest that was usually won by someone living in the prestigious community at the top of Highway 269, not far from Quail Springs at the base of Mingus Mountain.

Jessica's mother, Cindy, knew they'd never have enough money to compare with the decorating in Quail Springs, but they decorated all the same.

At least they used to.

As Christmas drew near, it was clear to everyone in the Warner home that this year would be different. And so, when the garland was strung up along Main Street, Jessica began to pray a special prayer out loud in her bed at night. Long after saying good night and being tucked into bed—separately—by her parents, Jessica would close her eyes and raise one hand high above her head, reaching out to God. "Dear God," she would whisper, "I'm not telling Mommy and Daddy about this, so please listen good. It's Christmastime and that's when you listen really hard to little girls' prayers. My teacher told me so. My prayer is this, God: please make Mommy and Daddy love each other again."

33

Though they were no longer churchgoers and prayer was something forgotten in the Warner home, little Jessica prayed the same prayer every night that season. And in that way, she was like many boys and girls in many homes all across the country praying for their parents to love each other.

But Jessica was also very different. This precious one could neither run nor skip nor hopscotch with her girlfriends. She could not jump rope or play hide-and-seek or run three-legged races.

She couldn't even walk.

Jessica had cerebral palsy.

It was something the townspeople of Cottonwood both knew and understood. Something that made them protective of little Jessica, causing them to go out of their way to wave at her in the aisles of Smith's Market or tousle her beautiful blonde curls as they passed and remind her that only angels were as pretty as she was.

Jessica was something of a fixture around Cottonwood, and the people who lived there felt richer for her presence. The child was too young to understand all of that, but Cottonwood was her home, her town. And Steve and Cindy Warner knew their daughter wouldn't want to live anywhere else for all the world.

34

That year, sometime after the garland was hung, Jessica asked her mother why her legs didn't work the same as those of other children. Cindy bent down and hugged her daughter close, her chest trembling as she tried to control the tears that welled up at the question. Gently, she helped Jessica to the living room sofa.

"I'd like to tell you a story, okay, honey?" Cindy ran her hand over Jessica's silky hair.

The little girl nodded and clutched more tightly to her Molly doll. "A story about me, Mommy?"

Cindy blinked back tears. "Yes, Jessie, a story about you. About what happened when you were born."

Then Cindy told her daughter of how she had been born a little too soon, before she was ready. Doctors had tried to stop Cindy from delivering but it was no use, and Jessica Marie was born ten weeks early, fighting for every breath. Three months later, when she had gained enough weight to go home, it was with this warning from her doctor: "I'm quite certain Jessica has some cerebral palsy. This is not something she will outgrow; but it is something that can be worked with."

Cindy paused. "You're very special, Jessica. God told me so himself the day he gave you to me."

The rest of the story Cindy kept to herself. How for that first year Steve and Cindy had refused to talk about their fears, and how they'd blamed Jessica's low birth weight when she didn't roll over or sit up or crawl like other babies her age. How in the days and months and years since then they'd anchored deep on opposite sides of Jessica's health issues.

35

The truth was they'd stopped taking Jessica to church after her first birthday only to avoid the curious comments and questions from their friends.

That was the year Steve purchased a pair of pink ballet slippers and hung them on a hook above Jessica's crib. "You're my perfect little princess," he whispered to the sleeping child. "And one day you'll dance across the room for me, won't you, honey?"

But doctors assured the Warners there would be no dancing for Jessica. The cerebral palsy did not affect her mind, but her motor skills were severely lacking. She would be doing well to be using a walker by the time she entered kindergarten.

When it became clear how great Jessica's handicap

was, Cindy quit her job to stay home and work with her daughter. She helped the child through hours of stretching routines and exercises, and both mother and child were often exhausted by the end of day.

"You're wasting your time," Steve would tell her. "She doesn't need all that work, Cindy. She's going to outgrow this thing. Wait and see."

And so they remained. Cindy's days were spent helping Jessica live with cerebral palsy. Steve's were spent denying she had it. Worst of all, in the midst of their miserable lives, their love for God grew cold and distant. In time the only member of the Warner household who listened to Bible stories and prayed to Jesus was Jessica, who after her second birthday went to church each Sunday with her grandparents.

The years had passed slowly and in all the ways Steve and Cindy could see, Jessica made little improvement. Days before her fifth birthday, she learned to spread her knees wide and crawl across the floor in a series of short, jerky motions. It was a victory, no matter how small, and Steve and Cindy shared Jessica's excitement.

"That's my girl," Steve told her. "One day you'll outgrow that cerebral palsy and wear those ballet slippers."

But that night after Jessica was asleep Cindy broke down and cried. "Her progress is so slow," she admitted. "I've done all the exercises, all the stretches. I've watched her diet and read every book on the subject. I've done everything I can. Why isn't she making more improvements?"

"I've told you, Cindy. You have to be patient. She'll outgrow this thing when she gets older."

"She'll never outgrow it, Steve," Cindy screamed at him. "If we work with her she can make progress. But you're never going to come through that door one night and find her dancing in those silly ballet slippers. Don't you understand?"

Steve didn't understand, and after that their lives grew even more separate. They communicated only when necessary and began socializing in separate circles. Cindy joined a cerebral palsy support group and finally found the understanding she'd been missing. The members of the support group did not deny Jessica's problems but rather brainstormed with her for solutions.

37

Meanwhile, Steve had been given a promotion and with it the task of organizing after-work events. His office friends were cheerful and upbeat, and Steve was often the life of the party. He liked them because they did not know about Jessica's cerebral palsy and so they never talked about muscle coordination or support groups or daily exercises.

Often, entire weeks went by where Steve and Cindy saw each other only minutes at a time, silently passing each other like strangers in the hallways of the Warner home.

It was in her fourth year that Jessica had noticed something was wrong with her mommy and daddy. They didn't kiss and hug and hold hands like other parents. And by this Christmas, Jessica knew there was only one answer. So each night before she fell asleep, Jessica would whisper her simple prayer, asking God to make her mommy and daddy love each other. But it hadn't seemed to make a difference.

Finally, two weeks before Christmas, Steve took Cindy's hand gently in his own and studied her face. "It isn't working between us, is it?" he asked her.

Tears sprang to Cindy's eyes, but her gaze remained calmly fixed on Steve's. "No, I guess it isn't."

"I'll talk to a divorce lawyer," Steve said gently. "But let's wait until after Christmas. For Jessica's sake."

As with most children, Jessica could tell things were worse between her parents. She talked it over with Molly, her beloved dolly. "I'm asking God to make them love each other," she said. "But they aren't very nice to each other anymore. I'm scared, Molly. Really scared."

At dinner one night, Jessica broke the silence. "Please, can we all go to church together this Sunday?" she asked. "Preacher's going to tell the Christmas story, and he said the whole family's invited."

Steve and Cindy exchanged a cool glance and then looked away, embarrassed. Steve cleared his throat. "Yes, sweetheart, that'll be fine," he said. "We'll all go to church together this Sunday. Like a family."

When Sunday came, they dressed Jessica in a white satin dress and sat beside her for the first time in years. The service was put on by all the Christian churches in town and held at the high school auditorium as it was each year at that time. The message was of hope and joy, the story of the Christ child born to a weary world so that men might live forevermore. It was a message that was tried and true, and in their private prisons of pain Steve and Cindy quietly realized the mistake they'd made by walking away from their faith.

"God gave the greatest gift of all, the gift of pure love wrapped in flesh and bones, the gift of his Son," the minister's voice rang clear. "But what of you? What will you give to the Savior this year?"

There was silence in the auditorium.

Tentatively, Steve ran a single finger along Jessica's stiff legs.

"I urge you," the pastor added quietly, "to take time these next few days and lay something at the Savior's feet. Something you love . . . or something you need to leave behind. Perhaps something that should have been laid there a long time ago."

On the way home that morning, Jessica turned to her father. "Did you hear him, Daddy?" she asked. "He said love is the greatest gift of all."

"Sure, honey," Steve said, staring straight ahead at the road in front of him.

"That's what I'm getting for you and Mommy this year," she announced merrily. "A whole lot of love."

Jessica thought a moment and then continued. "Preacher also said to give something to Jesus, something you love very much. Isn't that right, Mommy?"

"That's right, honey."

Steve and Cindy forgot about Jessica's conversation until the next morning as they were getting ready for the day. First Steve, then Cindy spotted something near the nativity scene set up on the living room floor. It was

39

Molly, Jessica's precious baby doll. She had laid it tenderly at the feet of the baby Jesus.

That afternoon while Steve was at the office, Cindy studied Jessica as she napped. What was the point of the pastor's message? she wondered. If love was such a great gift, how come her marriage was dissolving? How come Jessica had cerebral palsy? The child loved God enough to give him her Molly doll. But what had God ever done for her, for any of them?

Cindy returned to the main room and sat alone listening to the haunting sounds of Christmas carols on the radio. She wanted to believe, but still the thought remained. What had the Christ child ever done for them?

When Steve returned late that night, Cindy was already in bed. But before he slipped under the sheets next to her, she felt him do something he hadn't done in months. He leaned over and gently kissed her good night.

The next day was Christmas Eve, and Steve was gone to work when Cindy woke up. She climbed out of bed, fixed breakfast for Jessica, and led her through two hours of stretches and exercises. Only then, just before lunchtime, did she again notice something unusual about the nativity scene. Molly's doll was gone, and now a manila envelope lay at the foot of the manger.

Curious, Cindy approached it and took the envelope in her hands. There on the outside were these words scribbled in Steve's handwriting.

"Lord, I have something to lay at your feet. Something I love very much. I give you my word: from now

40

on I will accept Jessica as she is. I have been horribly un-
fair to my family by pretending she will one day be different than who you made her to be. I understand now.
Jessica can only learn to live with her cerebral palsy if I
learn to live with it first." Cindy opened the package, and
there, inside, were the unused pink ballet slippers that
had hung on Jessica's wall for four years.

Cindy curved her fingers around the slippers and allowed the tears to come. She cried because her little girl
would never wear them, never dance as her father had
once dreamed. But she also cried because if Steve was finally ready to accept the truth, then maybe he was ready
to work with her and not against her. Maybe there was
hope after all.

She wiped her eyes and looked at the carved figurine
of the Christ child, and suddenly the answer to her question became clear. Jesus had given them himself. Because
of him they could learn to love again. With him they
could survive as a family. And through him they could
live eternally in a place where Jessica could run and play
and jump with the other children.

Cindy fell to her knees and hung her head. "Forgive
me, Lord." And as she stayed there, she began to wonder
what a flawed woman like herself could give to one so
holy.

Her tears slowed and quietly she tiptoed into Jessica's
room and watched her napping. This time she felt no bit-
terness toward God as she studied the small girl. Golden
ringlets softly framed her pretty face and Cindy saw only
peace and contentment there as deep in her heart a light

dawned. In that moment, with all her being, she was absolutely certain about what she would give to Jesus.

That night when Steve came home, the house was dark but for the lights around the nativity scene. He studied the figurines standing around the Christ child and saw that his envelope was gone. In its place was a smaller white one. Steve crossed the room, set down his overcoat and briefcase, and slid a finger under the flap. Inside was a single sheet of paper and something small wrapped in tissue paper. Steve read the handwritten note with tears in his eyes.

"Dear Lord, I give back to you what you—five years ago—gave to me. I have held on too tightly, Lord, forgotten that this precious gift was never really mine. I let another child take the place of the one that lay in a hay-filled manger that cold night in Bethlehem. And now love has all but died in our home. I'm sorry, Lord. I've tried to make her something other than what you made her, but no more. I'll love her always, but I understand now that she doesn't belong to me. She belongs to you. Now and forevermore."

Steve unwrapped the tissue paper, and there inside lay a single small picture of Jessica.

Steve heard something and turned. With Jessica perched on her hip, Cindy was watching him from the doorway. Her eyes glistened with unshed tears and Steve went to her, hugging her tightly as Jessica wrapped her arms around them both.

"We can't throw it all away. Not when we haven't

even tried," he whispered. "I'm ready to work with you, Cindy."

She nodded, choking back a sob. "All my efforts and all your denial and we almost missed the truth," she said. "When she put Molly at Jesus' feet . . . Steve, she's perfect just the way she is. She loves more perfectly than either of us ever has. She reminded me of all God has done for me, for all of us."

"That's her Christmas gift to us, right, sweetheart?" Steve lifted Jessica's chin and kissed her forehead.

Jessica nodded and grinned, first at her daddy and then at the tiny statue of baby Jesus in the nativity scene. She did not understand everything that had happened between her parents and the Lord that Christmas. Only that the town of Cottonwood felt a little like heaven that week because her prayers had been answered. The preacher had been right.

43

Love really was the best Christmas miracle of all.

A Touch of
Heaven

*N*ewly married and fresh out of Bible college, Ashley and Bill Larson began making plans to be missionaries in Africa. They spent that next year taking training courses on the African diet, socialization process, and other important details that would aid them in their four-year stint on another continent.

When they had nearly completed their education and had already been assigned to a village in a remote tribal area, Bill had an idea. He had been trained in Bible education and knew well the message he and Ashley would present to the tribal people. But he had never studied the power of healing through prayer.

"I think I'm going to take that course," Bill told his wife one afternoon.

Ashley nodded and shrugged her shoulders. "Why not?"

The two discussed the course, and Ashley, pregnant with their first child, decided she would not have time for the additional work. But Bill was intrigued. If he was going to tell the people about God's love, then he'd better be prepared to tell them about his healing power as well.

Although raised in the Christian church and well versed in scripture, Bill had never thought much of the preachers who did healing demonstrations. Many of them had proved to be frauds over the years. Even worse, a number had been swindlers who only performed trickery in exchange for donations. And so to consider the true healing nature of God was a new idea for Bill.

He began the class at about the same time that Ashley visited a doctor for what had become a persistent lower and middle back pain.

"I'm afraid I have bad news for you, Mrs. Larson," the doctor told her as the two sat in his office after her examination. "The X rays show that you're suffering from the early stages of scoliosis."

The doctor went on to explain that scoliosis was a disease that caused the spine to begin to curve unnaturally, forcing the body to become severely hunched and causing excruciating pain in its victims. When the disease occurs in children, it can be managed with a series of braces since the child's skeletal frame is still growing. However, when it strikes an adult, there is nothing that can be done.

"What can I expect?" Ashley asked, fighting tears. The news was devastating. She and Bill had so many plans for the future. If she were going to be strong enough to bear children and live the rugged life of a missionary in Africa, she would need a healthy back.

"The pain you're experiencing will get worse. Within the next two years you will be able to notice the curving in your spine. I'm sorry."

Ashley nodded in resignation and returned home to share the news with Bill. He sympathized with her and then told her his own news. He had met twice already with the class on healing through prayer. He told her he was impressed with the stories he was hearing. Not stories of tent revival healings or televised miracles, but quiet stories of health changes that in his opinion could be nothing less than modern-day miracles. Christmas was two days away, and suddenly Bill was overwhelmed by the presence of God in their lives. How could they doubt for a minute that the Lord could heal, could work a miracle? And what better time to ask for a miracle than Christmas week? When the greatest miracle of all had happened two thousand years ago.

That night as they were falling asleep, Bill sat up in bed and spoke to Ashley in the dark of their room.

"Would you mind if I pray for your back, Ashley?"

Ashley shrugged, already partially asleep. "Sure. Do I have to move?"

"No. You're fine."

Ashley was lying on her side, a position that favored her painful back. As she lay, falling asleep, Bill spent thirty minutes holding his hands above her back and praying silently that God would heal her condition.

Each night during that Christmas week, he continued this routine. Just as they were about to go to sleep, he would sit up, place his hands over Ashley's back, and pray specifically for God to heal her scoliosis. On the seventh night, something strange happened.

Bill had been praying for his wife for ten minutes when suddenly he spoke.

"Ashley?"

"Yes?" She was still awake.

"Do you feel anything?"

"Just your hand moving up and down along my spine."

Bill's eyes widened in surprise. "Ashley, I haven't touched your back."

Ashley sat up quickly and turned to look at Bill. "That's not funny!"

Bill shook his head. "I'm serious, Ashley. I haven't touched you. The only reason I asked if you felt something was because I had my hand over your back and at that moment I was feeling something warm beneath my hand."

"What do you think it was?"

"I don't know. But I'm going to keep praying."

Ashley yawned and lay back down on their bed. "It can't hurt. Besides, I know God could heal me if he wanted to. I just don't know if that's part of his plan for us. Modern miracles and all."

"By the way, how's your pain?" Bill asked.

Ashley paused a moment and then sat upright once more. "You know, actually I can't feel it."

There was silence between them for a moment as they considered the warmth that had passed along Ashley's back and the feeling of a human hand moving up and down her spine.

"Do you think," Ashley asked quietly, "I might be healed?"

"I think we need to see how you feel tomorrow and in the meantime keep praying."

Two weeks later, after Ashley and Bill had flown to Pennsylvania to visit her parents, she saw a doctor who had known her as a child. She brought with her the X rays and diagnosis from the previous doctor. Upon initial examination of the records, the doctor agreed with the diagnosis: severe scoliosis, which appeared to be progressing rapidly.

Then, upon Ashley's request, the doctor took another set of X rays and performed an additional examination of her spine.

"I don't know how to explain this," the doctor said as he reentered the examination room. "Ashley, there's no sign of scoliosis at all. Your back is perfectly normal."

Ashley was stunned. She remembered the night when she had felt a hand moving gently along her back. "Could it somehow have reversed itself?" she asked the doctor, wanting to be absolutely sure about what had happened.

"No. For a person to have scoliosis as severely as you did in these last X rays"—the doctor held the photographs up to the light and shook his head—"you would definitely have had scar tissue, even if it had somehow reversed itself."

"Then how do you explain it?"

The doctor put the films gently on a nearby table and smiled at Ashley. "I've learned over the years that there are some things we on Earth cannot explain when it comes to medical healings. I like to call them miracles."

Ashley shared with the doctor the incident weeks earlier when at Christmastime Bill had been praying and she had felt a hand on her spine at the same time that he felt a warmth passing beneath his hand. To Ashley's surprise, the doctor nodded.

"Yes, when we hear of this type of thing—and we don't hear about it very often—there is often a warmth associated with it. It doesn't take a lot of believing on my part. After all, the human body itself is a working miracle. That our Creator would continue to work miracles within us is in my opinion quite possible."

Months later when Ashley and Bill left for Africa, it was in good health and with a deep respect for the kind of prayer that God answers in the form of miraculous healing. And a feeling of intense gratitude for the Lord's two special Christmas gifts: Ashley's healthy spine, and the ability to go into the mission believing that what the Bible says is true: Nothing is impossible with God.

Home for Christmas

*B*arbara Oliver was the only one of her five siblings who never quite fit in. When her four sisters played sports with their only brother, she watched on the sidelines. When the girls grew older and began dating, Barbara stayed at home and watched television; she felt too shy and unlovely to mix with the boys her age.

She struggled with her weight and often sat alone at family get-togethers, feeling too self-conscious to participate. And so her peers and even her immediate family often forgot about her, finding it easier to involve themselves in their own lives than to take time to figure out why Barbara was so quiet.

During those crucial formative years, Barbara appeared to have few opinions and even fewer social graces, but inside her lived a young woman nearly bursting with the desire to be loved and cared for. For that reason, from the time she was old enough to walk, she idolized the two men in her life: her brother, Lou, and her father, Hank.

Hank Oliver was a small-town doctor during the years when his family was growing up in Glenview, Illinois. He was the type of practitioner who still made house calls and who allowed his patients to pay him by whatever means they could—even if that meant trading a handpicked bag of produce for one of his visits. He had the lowest charges in town, and while most doctors would only prescribe medications, he was willing to teach people nutrition and preventative measures for improving their health.

Everyone in town loved Doctor Hank, as they called him. The feeling was mutual, and he often spent seven days a week engulfed in his practice. Just a handful of people in Glenview ever wondered if Doctor Hank loved them in return, and they lived under his roof.

"Don't you ever wonder, Lou?" Barbara asked her brother one day when they were in their early teens. "He's gone so much of the time that I'm not sure whether he really loves us or not."

Lou's eyes fell, and he stared at the baseball and glove in his hands. His father had promised to play ball with him that day, but once again he'd been called away for a medical emergency.

"Yeah," he said after a while. "I know what you mean. If he loves us, then why can't he spend more time with us? It seems like he should want to be with us more than with his patients."

Hank was such a happy, good-natured man that the children felt foolish voicing any complaints at all except to each other. But still they missed their father and once in a while continued to wonder about how much he loved them.

Time passed, and Hank's health declined rapidly. He had been diagnosed years before with a disease that made him prone to seizures. But it wasn't until ten years later that he began degenerating and finally had to give up his practice.

He finally succumbed to his illness after making peace with each of his children. Throughout the final days of his life, it was often Barbara and Lou who took turns waiting on him and comforting him.

"What are we going to do without him?" Barbara asked her brother not long after the funeral. "I can't imagine living in a world where he's not around."

Lou nodded. Their family had been raised to love God and obey the Bible. He knew that his father was in heaven. But still, the pain of losing him was almost too much to bear. Especially after coming to understand in his father's final years just how much the man loved him.

"I don't know, Barbara," he said, putting an arm around her shoulders. "But I know that what Dad taught us is true. He's in heaven, and one day we'll go to live with him there and we'll all be together again. What a homecoming that'll be, huh?"

Barbara smiled through her tears. "Yeah, and in heaven he won't have to make house calls."

In the decade that followed, although the rest of Barbara's siblings all went their own ways, Barbara became very attached to her brother, Lou. Shortly after Lou joined the Navy, she, too, joined. When Lou finished serving his time, he married, taught college, and eight years later moved to San Diego, where he began working on his second master's degree at the University of San Diego.

After serving a double hitch in the Navy, Barbara also moved to San Diego and found a house just a few miles from Lou's. She, too, began attending the university.

Lou worried about his sister's lack of independence. "I know she wants to get married and have a family of her own," he confided to his wife, Anna, one day. "But all she does is go to school, work, and sit home, in front of the television set. She can't expect to meet someone living like that."

Anna angled her head thoughtfully. "I think it's just going to take more time with Barbara. She's starting to come out of her shell some, and once she has her degree she'll feel a lot better about things. Don't worry about her."

Besides, it wasn't as if Barbara didn't have a family. She did. Over the next fifteen years, Lou and Anna raised four children, and Barbara was always at the center of their family outings.

Over time, Barbara earned a bachelor's degree in rehabilitation and began working in an alcohol-recovery center. Her patients ranged from hopeless adults to troubled teens, and Barbara worked tirelessly with them.

As Barbara became more involved with her patients, Lou and Anna began to notice a change in her.

"You know," Lou said one night as he and his wife washed dinner dishes together at the kitchen sink, "all of us kids growing up used to think there was something wrong with Barbara. We thought she'd never amount to much, I guess because she was so alone and never did the things the rest of us did."

54

He paused a moment before continuing. "But that isn't true at all. She's got her education and a wonderful job. She gives hope to people who have none, and for dozens of her patients she's the greatest gift God has ever given them."

"I told you, Lou," Anna said warmly. "You used to worry so much about Barbara."

"I still worry about her because she has no family of her own. All she's ever really wanted is a family."

"She's growing at her own pace." Anna smiled, drying her hands on a nearby towel and setting it back on the countertop. "For now, though, it's not like she has no one. We're her family. But one of these days, when she's ready, she will meet the right person and then she'll have her family. She has plenty of time yet. Watch and see."

But a few years later, Barbara was diagnosed with breast cancer. At forty-three, she was younger than most breast cancer patients, so doctors were at first hopeful she might survive. They removed a cancerous section of her breast, and when the cancer continued to spread, they performed a mastectomy. The surgery was followed up by chemotherapy and radiation treatments, which caused Barbara's hair to fall out and often left her violently ill.

Still, she continued to work, staying home only on the days when she felt sickest. When she was at work, she put her personal troubles behind her and concentrated only on helping her patients.

"That woman is amazing," Anna said one day as she watched Barbara making dinner for her family in the kitchen.

Lou stared thoughtfully at his sister. "She's a fighter, all right. But I'm so worried about her."

"The cancer?"

Lou nodded. "She talked to the doctor yesterday. It's spread into her lymph system."

Anna hung her head and sighed, and for a long time neither of them said anything. There was no need. They both knew what the news meant. When cancer spreads through the lymph system, as it had in Barbara's body, the outcome was too often certain.

That was in the spring, but Barbara continued to work through the first part of November before succumbing to her illness and taking a leave of absence. The cancer had continued to spread, this time beyond her lymph system into her entire body, and doctors did not expect her to live more than six months.

Now, when Lou visited Barbara at her apartment, their time together was painful for both of them.

"You've got to hang in here and pull through this," Lou would tell her as he sat at the edge of her bed and helped her take sips of ice water. She had lost a lot of weight and her skin looked gray and lifeless.

"I'm trying, Lou, really I am," she would say, never complaining about the effort it took to muster her strength.

When Lou would leave Barbara's apartment, he would often bow his head and pray before driving home.

"Lord, please help me see Barbara through this terrible disease. I pray that she lives. But if her time has come to go home to you, I pray you make the transition easy. Please don't let her suffer, Lord."

Throughout November and much of December, Lou got off work early and stopped to visit Barbara. Although her body was obviously deteriorating, she was not bedridden, and Lou was thankful for that. After their visits he would normally return home for dinner and then go back to see Barbara later in the evening, sometimes bringing her a plate of whatever they'd eaten that night.

"It's getting to me, Anna," he confided to his wife one morning. "I hate to see her falling apart. One of these days she's going to be too weak to get off the couch, and then what are we going to do?"

Anna thought a moment. "Well, we could have her come live with us."

Lou had thought of the possibility, but knew it would be difficult to make it work. Each of their three bedrooms was being used, and there wouldn't be anyone home during the day to take care of Barbara. Still, he wanted her to feel welcome. If there was any way they could figure out the logistics, having Barbara come live with them was really the only option Lou could imagine.

That week—two weeks before Christmas—he told Barbara about the idea.

"No way, Lou. Not on your life," she said, trying to sound firm. "You and Anna and the kids have been my family for such a long time; you've done so much for me." She continued, struggling with each word because of her weakened condition. "I'm not going to impose on you now and make you change your whole house around just so I can come there to die."

"Barbara, don't talk like that," Lou chided her gently. "You're going to pull through this. You've had hard times before, but you've always fought it. I want you home for Christmas so you can turn the corner on this thing and get better."

But both brother and sister knew there was no truth in his words. That much was clear as Christmas drew nearer and Barbara finally became unable to leave her bed except for a brief period once or twice each day.

"Listen, Barbara, if you won't come live with me and Anna, then you need to move to the Veterans' Hospice or someplace where you can have help around the clock," Lou said. "It's eating me up knowing you're here alone and going through so much pain by yourself. Especially at Christmastime."

"I'm fine," Barbara insisted. "I can reach my medication, and I have water by me all the time. I get meals delivered to me and whatever you bring me. That's plenty of food. I don't need any help."

Lou disagreed, and his sister's situation weighed heavily on him. He prayed that afternoon about a solution for Barbara's living arrangements, asking God to show him what to do for her.

"God, you know her heart, and I pray you convince her to give up her independence. She needs help, Lord, and I can't provide it all. I don't want her living alone, so please help us to work things out. Help her to be willing to move if that's what is necessary. Amen."

58

Finally, one afternoon later that week, Lou left a message for Barbara's doctor, Dr. Sylvia Sanchez, to call him. He planned to ask the doctor to have a talk with Barbara. Maybe she could convince Barbara that she needed to leave her apartment and get help.

The next morning, December 22, Dr. Sanchez returned Lou's call.

"Yes, this is Barbara's brother, Lou," he said.

"Hello, Lou. We're all very fond of Barbara," she said politely. "How can I help you?"

"First of all, I think she's getting worse very quickly and I'm concerned about her," he said.

"She's lost some mobility," Dr. Sanchez explained.

"But I still think she's got another three months or more."

"That's why I'm calling. See, I've asked her to come live with me and my family, but she won't do it. She thinks she'll be in the way, and I haven't been able to change her mind." Lou drew in a deep breath. "I called because I was hoping you might be able to talk some sense into her. If she won't come live with me, she needs to be at a hospice or a group home, someplace where she can have help around the clock."

Dr. Sanchez thought for a moment before responding. "Have you considered helping her move in with your father?" she asked.

Lou's face twisted in confusion; he was not sure he had heard the doctor correctly. "What?"

"Maybe it's time she go and live with your father," the doctor repeated. "Sometime around October, I got a call from your father. He wanted to know how she was doing, and he seemed very knowledgeable about her particular case. I was surprised and asked him if he was a doctor, which he said he was. Seemed odd to me that Barbara had never mentioned it before. Anyway, we chatted for a few minutes. Before we finished talking, he told me he'd never gotten to spend enough time with Barbara when she was a little girl." The doctor hesitated. "He told me that when things got really bad, people shouldn't worry about Barbara because she would be going home to live with him at Christmas."

Lou had no idea what to say.

"Mr. Oliver? Are you there?"

Lou cleared his throat. "Dr. Sanchez, my father died many years ago. There's no way he could have made that phone call."

"How strange," she said. "Wait. Just a minute." There was a rustling sound of paper as Dr. Sanchez located Barbara's file.

"Okay, here it is. Let me see. Yes, it's right here. On October fifteenth I received a call on my cell phone from a Dr. Hank Oliver. The man said he was Barbara's father and that when she got toward the end of her illness she'd be going home to live with him."

Lou shook his head, trying to make sense of the situation. "That's fine, Dr. Sanchez, but my father's been dead for almost thirty years. Obviously he couldn't make a phone call."

60

"Is it possible it was an uncle or some other relative or friend?" she asked. "As I said, the man was very knowledgeable about Barbara and her condition. Is there another doctor in your family? I never mentioned the call to Barbara because I assumed your father had discussed it with her before calling me."

There was silence between them again. "Doctor, you're sure the man said he was Barbara's father?"

"Definitely. I remember the call very clearly. I'm sure it must have been an uncle or something. Either way, why don't you look into it and let me know. It sounds like somewhere there's a family member who is expecting her to come home to live with him. Meanwhile I'll work on Barbara and try to convince her that it isn't wise for her to be alone anymore."

"I'd like her home with us before Christmas, Doctor."

"Don't worry; I'll call her this afternoon."

Lou hung up the phone and sat staring at it, wondering who would have made such a strange call. There were several uncles in the Oliver family, but none of them knew Barbara very well, and certainly none of them would have identified themselves as Barbara's father. Nevertheless, he spent much of the day contacting every male relative who knew Barbara and asking if anyone had called Barbara's doctor. By that evening he had learned that none of them knew anything about it.

Suddenly he remembered his prayer. He had asked God to work out Barbara's living arrangements, and now he had discovered that Dr. Sanchez had received a phone call from someone claiming to be Hank Oliver. Was it possible that God had answered his prayers by letting him know that Barbara was eventually going to be going home to heaven, where she would be reunited with their father?

Lou told Anna what had happened, and she, too, thought it might be possible. Perhaps, she said, the phone call was God's way of letting them know Barbara was headed for a better place.

"But that doesn't help us right now," she added. "We still don't know where she needs to be for the next three months until she dies. Christmas is in two days. She needs a place to live, Lou."

"I know. That's the strange part. If it's an answer to

61

prayer, then what do we do about the next three months?"

The answer came too quickly.

Early on Christmas Eve—the day after Barbara agreed to go home with Lou and Anna—she died peacefully in her sleep. She had been completely bedridden for just two days.

Dr. Sanchez and the others were baffled when they heard the news. Although she had been very clearly dying, they thought Barbara should have had at least another three months to live.

At the Oliver home, Barbara's death sent Lou and Anna on a roller-coaster ride of mixed emotions.

"I'm going to miss her so much," Lou said, his eyes brimming with tears. "But she was no longer able to live alone, and God knew it was time for her to come home. Home for Christmas . . ."

"It makes you wonder, doesn't it?" Anna asked.

Lou raised an eyebrow. "About the phone call, you mean? Yeah, it does. The more I think about it, the more I believe it just might have been Dad making that phone call."

"Maybe so."

"Really," Lou continued. "I believe God wanted us to know everything was going to work out fine. Barbara wouldn't need a place to live because she was going home to heaven."

Anna was silent, lost in her own thoughts.

"You know something, Anna?" Lou said. "I always wondered if Dad really loved me. Barbara wondered the

62

same thing. But now I feel like I can put that behind me. God knew that I wondered about my dad. So he answered my prayer and let me know that Dad did love both of us. He loved us so much that he was looking forward to welcoming the first of his children home."

A Gift for Noel

*B*y the time Noel Conover had her first birthday, her parents, Evan and Susie, began to notice something different about her. She was silent. Whereas other children her age might coo or say simple words, Noel rarely uttered any sound at all.

Finally her parents arranged an appointment with a specialist who confirmed their fears. Noel had been born deaf and would remain so for the rest of her life. On the drive home from the doctor's office, Noel sat in the backseat playing with a stuffed animal while Evan and Susie held hands and shared their grief over the news.

"I want so much for her to be like the other

kids," Susie said, wiping the tears from her cheeks. "It just isn't fair. She's such a beautiful girl, and now she's going to be different from her peers for the rest of her life. When I think of all the sounds she'll miss . . . She'll never hear me say her name or sing her a lullaby."

Evan stared straight ahead, keeping his eyes on the road. "I keep thinking that she'll never hear me tell her how much I love her." He glanced at his wife. "She'll never hear any of it."

Susie and Evan vowed that day to always be strong for Noel and to expect only the best from her in every situation. They would never allow her to use deafness as an excuse for doing anything less than she was capable of. They agreed to learn sign language and to teach Noel as soon as possible. And they would also teach her to read lips so that she would have an easier time fitting in with other children in a school setting. They knew there would be times of disappointment and setbacks, but they promised to lean on each other and give Noel the best life possible despite her handicap.

As the years passed, the Conovers lived up to their promise. While she was still a toddler, Noel learned to speak to her parents in sign language, and soon she was making progress in her ability to read lips.

Teaching Noel to make friends with hearing children proved to be the most difficult aspect of helping her learn to live with her deafness. As a toddler, Noel was introduced to lots of children her age but never seemed to fit in with them. Once while at the park, she tried to talk in sign language to a young girl who was obviously able to hear.

"Want to play with my dolly?" Noel signed quickly.

The child gave Noel a blank stare and looked at her hands. "Why are you moving your hands like that?" the girl asked.

Noel looked at the girl curiously, unable to understand her lip movements, and then once again used sign language to ask the girl if she wanted to play. This time the child began to laugh at Noel, assuming that Noel was playing some kind of game.

But the girl's laughter confused Noel and she began to cry, turning and running to where her mother sat painfully watching the exchange from a nearby park bench.

"It's all right," Susie signed to her daughter, taking her into her arms. "She wants to be your friend, honey. She just didn't understand you."

"She didn't like me," Noel signed back to her mother. Susie's heart went out to her daughter, whose tiny spirit seemed crushed by the encounter.

"No," Susie signed in return. "She liked you. She just didn't understand you."

But Noel seemed frightened, and Susie thought she knew why. For the first time the little girl understood that she was different from other children, and the thought must have terrified her. After that, Noel refused to make any attempt to communicate with other children. She would play near them and smile at them, but she always remained an outsider.

A Gift for Noel

"What are we going to do, Evan?" a weary Susie complained one night. "I've tried to help her make friends with the other children, but she's afraid to make an effort, afraid they won't like her."

"Give it time, honey," Evan said, sitting down at the table across from his wife. "She has a lot of adjusting to do, and she's come so far in such a few years. She'll have friends one day."

Susie was quiet for a moment. "Evan," she finally said softly. "Have you prayed about it? I mean the friendship thing?"

Evan looked sad as he answered. "Not really. I mean, of course I've prayed for Noel. I've prayed for her since the day she was born. But I haven't really asked God to send her a special friend, if that's what you mean."

Susie nodded. "Well, let's do it. Let's pray together and then let's keep praying every day that God will love Noel enough to send her a special friend."

Evan reached across the table and took Susie's hands. Together they bowed their heads and prayed. Quietly, sincerely, they asked that Noel be watched over and cared for and that God would find it in his heart to give Noel a special friend.

After that, Evan and Susie prayed daily for Noel and the friend she might one day have. Later that year, Noel turned five and began attending a school for children with special needs. Academically she excelled far beyond her parents' dreams, but she still struggled socially.

One day she came home with her head high and,

67

much as an adult would, asked her mother to sit with her on the couch and talk for a while.

"I'm deaf, right, Mommy?" she signed.

Susie paused a moment. They had dealt with Noel's deafness since the day she was diagnosed, but they had never discussed with her exactly what made her different from other children. "Yes, honey." Susie moved her hands gently, her eyes searching her daughter's. "You were born without the ability to hear sound."

"And that makes me different, right, Mommy?" she asked.

Susie sighed, feeling the tears well up in her eyes. "Yes, honey. Most children can hear sounds. But there are many children who were born deaf, just like you."

"Even though I'm deaf, I'm still smart and I'm still pretty, and I'm still special. Isn't that right, Mommy?" Noel's eyes shone as she asked the question, and Susie struggled to keep from crying. "And God still loves me, right?"

"Of course, Noel. God loves you very much. You are very special and beautiful and very wonderful, and being deaf will never change that."

Noel thought for a moment. Then her hands began to move once again. "It's time for me to have a friend, Mommy. But I want a friend who's deaf like me. Is that okay?"

Susie pulled her daughter close and wrapped her arms around the child, stroking her silky dark curls. "I've been asking God to send you a special friend, Noel.

A Gift for Noel

Maybe that's what he has in mind. A special friend who is deaf like you. We'll just have to wait and see."

The year ran its course, and although Noel made more of an attempt with the other children than she had in the past, none of her classmates was deaf, and she finished her first year of school without a close friend. Her second year started much the same way and though they were discouraged, Evan and Susie continued to pray.

Two months before Christmas, Noel stumbled upon a picture of a white Persian kitten, much like the one of her storybooks. She was immediately and completely enamored with the kitten and ran to show her mother the picture, her hands flying as she tried to explain herself.

"Mommy, can I please have a kitten like that for Christmas? Please?" Noel was so animated that Susie had to calm her down before her daughter would show her the picture in the book.

69

"That's a Persian kitten, Noel," Susie said as she looked at the picture. "You want a kitten like that?"

"Yes, yes, yes," Noel signed quickly. "Please, Mommy," she pleaded.

Later that night, Susie and Evan discussed the idea of getting Noel a kitten for Christmas.

"She's always loved her stuffed animals," Susie said as she presented the idea. "Maybe that's just what she needs right now. A pet of her own."

"But a white Persian kitten?" Evan asked. "They cost hundreds of dollars, Susie. You know we can't afford that."

Evan was a teacher and Susie worked part-time at

Noel's school. With the cost of their daughter's special education, they were barely able to scrape enough money together to meet monthly needs.

"I know," Susie said. "But maybe we could save for the next few weeks and watch the advertisements in the newspaper. Maybe there'll be one for sale that we can afford."

Evan thought a moment and sighed. "All right, let's try it. But don't say anything to Noel about it. I'd hate to get her hopes up."

For the next seven weeks Susie scanned the newspapers for white Persian kittens and found none for sale. Finally, a week before Christmas, she and Evan decided they had managed to save enough money to purchase such a kitten if only they could find one.

On December 23, while Noel was still sleeping, Susie opened the newspaper and pored over the classified advertisements. Suddenly she gasped out loud.

"Evan! They're here. The kittens. 'Persian kittens, white, $200.' Can you believe it! We've found Noel's kitten."

When Noel was up and playing in the other room, Susie dialed the number listed in the advertisement.

"Yes," she said when someone answered the phone. "I'm calling about the white Persian kittens."

On the other line Mary Jenkins smiled. "Oh, yes," she said. "We have a few left and they're the same, white kittens with gray markings."

"Oh." Susie's face fell in disappointment. "We were

looking for one that is completely white. It's for my daughter's Christmas present."

"I see," Mary said. "Well, there is one kitten that's completely white. I'll sell her to you for fifty dollars instead of the two hundred, if you're interested."

"I don't understand," Susie said, puzzled.

"Well"—Mary paused—"the kitten is deaf. I'm not sure if I'll be able to sell her."

Susie began to shake, and for a moment she was unable to speak. Noel entered the room and realized something strange was happening. "What, Mommy? What is it?" she began to sign.

"Are you still there?" Mary asked, breaking the silence.

"Yes! We'll be over in half an hour."

Susie hung up the phone and called Evan into the room. "Let's tell her," she said. "That way we can all go get the kitty together."

They explained that they had found a kitten for Noel . . . and that even though Christmas was two days away, they wanted Noel to have her pet that day.

Evan, Susie, and Noel met Mary on her front porch, and immediately Noel was drawn to the perfect white kitten in the woman's arms. "Snowball," Noel signed. And gently she took the baby cat in her arms, holding the tiny animal close to her chest.

Evan and Susie exchanged a glance. "Let's tell her," Susie mouthed the words and Evan nodded. Stooping to Noel's level, Susie quickly began moving her hands. "The kitten is a girl kitten, and it's deaf, Noel. A deaf white Persian kitten."

Noel's face lit up as Susie had never seen it do before. "She's my kitten, Mommy!" she signed.

They all smiled and Evan paid Mary for the kitten. As he did, she explained how the other kittens would run and hide when she ran the vacuum, but the white kitten seemed unaffected by the noise. Evan and Susie exchanged a knowing glance, remembering the days when they were trying to figure out what was wrong with Noel.

"Eventually I had the kitten checked by a veterinarian, and she told us the poor little thing was deaf," Mary told them.

Susie petted the kitten and then got Noel's attention. Her hands moving, she said, "See, Noel. She's perfect and beautiful and special, just like the other kittens. The only difference is she can't hear."

Noel smiled, snuggling her face up close to the kitten's. Then she looked at her mother and with her free hand said, "Let's take her home, Mommy."

Over the next few weeks there was no separating Noel and her tiny deaf kitten. Every afternoon she would set the kitten in front of her on her bed and use sign language to talk to her. One day Susie watched, trying to understand what Noel was telling the kitten.

"It's okay, Kitty," Noel said, her little hands moving slowly so her kitten could understand. "You don't have to be afraid or lonely anymore because now there's two deaf people in our family. You're the best Christmas present ever. We'll be best friends for always."

Susie walked into the room slowly and sat down next to Noel.

"You love her, don't you, Noel?" she signed to her daughter.

"Yes, Mommy. She and I are both special because we're both deaf." Noel looked at her kitten, whose soft white face was tilted curiously as she watched Noel's fingers move. Noel looked back at her mother. "She doesn't understand sign language yet, but when she gets older she will. And then it will be easier for her to talk to me."

Noel reached for the kitten and held her close. "Thank you for praying, Mommy. God heard your prayers," she signed. "He gave me a friend who was born deaf just like me. And at Christmastime, too!"

73

"Yes, Noel." Susie smiled. "I was just thinking that. God definitely heard our prayers. Your kitty is the best Christmas present of all."

The First Day
of Christmas

*C*ara Wilcox was anxious to get out of the house for a while. It was December 12—the first day of Christmas—and already the air was freezing cold outside. Life had been difficult for the Wilcox family lately and Cara had no idea how she'd afford Christmas. Times like that cool winter night, Cara knew the only way to get her mind off her worries was to get outside—even in their crowded neighborhood—and get some fresh air.

"Who wants to take a walk?" she asked as she climbed into her coat. It was very dark outside, and Cara's New York neighborhood was not very secure.

And that evening she planned to walk no more than once around the block.

Cara looked into the faces of her four children and saw that none of the older three was excited about the idea of a walk. Sarah, five, and Joey, seven, shook their heads.

"We want to watch TV, Mom," they said.

Cara looked at her oldest son, Colin, fifteen, and the boy shrugged. "Not tonight, Mom. Okay?"

"Sure," she said. "But you watch Joey and Sarah, all right? I'll take Laura."

Her three-year-old daughter had a lot of energy, and Cara found her riding toy. Even though it was cold, the child could ride alongside her for one block without it bothering her. It would be good for both of them. She took the child's hand, and together they left the apartment.

Once outside, Cara and Laura had not traveled far when the child no longer wanted her riding toy. Cara sighed and picked up the toy. As she did, she glanced behind her. She was only about half a block from home, and suddenly she saw Joey and Sarah walking up the street. They were acting sneaky, darting in and out of the shadows as if they were trying to catch up to their mother and surprise her, so Cara decided to play along.

Turning back toward the direction she'd been walking in, she and Laura continued down the street. When they reached the intersection, Cara turned around and looked for them again. This time she didn't see them.

"Hmm," she said out loud, and Laura looked up at her.

"C'mon, Mommy," the child said. "Walk."

Cara stood unmoving, staring back toward her house and straining to see the children. She wondered if perhaps they had gotten scared of the dark and decided to go back home. Then the thought occurred to her that perhaps someone had snatched them. The neighborhood was often a frightening place, and crimes were committed around them each day. Suddenly Cara began to panic.

"Sarah!" she called out. "Joey!"

There was no response, and Cara could feel herself actually shaking in fear. Quickly she turned around, tightened her grip on Laura's hand, and began heading back toward the apartment.

As they walked, Cara noticed a man across the street who was headed in the same direction. Cara wondered where he had come from, since the few times she had looked back to check her children, she hadn't noticed him. Although she was preoccupied with finding Joey and Sarah, Cara noticed that the man across the street kept looking at them. Since she did not recognize him as someone who lived in the neighborhood, Cara began to be suspicious of the man and picked up her pace, sweeping Laura into her arms. In one hand she held the riding toy and decided she would use it in self-defense if necessary.

"What's wrong, Mommy?" Laura asked, aware of her mother's nervousness.

"Nothing, honey. We're going home now."

As Cara and her daughter neared the corner of her apartment building, the man began crossing the street at an angle headed in their direction. Terror raced through Cara's body, and she wondered if she could reach her apartment in time if he tried to accost them.

At that instant a thought came to Cara.

Pretend you see your father at the front door and talk to him, a voice seemed to say.

Instantly Cara acted on the suggestion.

"Hi, Dad!" she yelled, waving in the direction of her apartment, still four units away. "Have you seen the kids?"

Almost at once the man who had been headed straight for her turned around and started walking in the opposite direction. Cara breathed a sigh of relief. She had tricked him into thinking that her father was really at the door.

Cara ran up her apartment steps and dashed inside. Her fears alleviated, Cara saw Joey and Sarah on the floor watching television as they had been when she left.

"Why'd you guys come back home?" she asked. "Did something scare you? What?"

The children looked blankly at their mother and then at each other. "What do you mean?" Joey asked.

"You were outside, following me. I saw you. Why'd you come back inside?"

Colin looked at his mother then and shook his head.

"Mom, they've been right here the whole time," he said simply. "They didn't want to go, remember?"

"That's impossible," she said, moving slowly toward

the chair. "I saw you both. Following behind us, and when I couldn't see you anymore, I turned around."

Then Cara remembered the strange man. For the next thirty minutes she tried to explain to Colin about the man and how threatened she had felt.

"Mom, maybe the kids you saw were angels and the only way they knew to get you to come back home was to make themselves look like Joey and Sarah. You know, Christmas angels."

Cara stared at her son. She had been thinking the same thing, but was afraid she'd sound crazy. But why not? Wouldn't it have been fitting for God to use angels who looked like her kids? Her precious children.

"I don't know, son. But I'm sure I saw the kids outside tonight."

Cara told everyone who would listen about the story of what happened on her walk, but it wasn't until later that she came to believe without a doubt that a miracle had occurred that night. It turned out that the man who had been trailing her was an escaped felon from the state prison. Until his recapture, he carried a gun, robbing people in Cara's neighborhood at gunpoint.

"I believe he intended to rob me, and then kill me and Laura," Cara told her friend later. "And by some Christmas miracle, God directed two children who looked just like mine to lead me back to safety while my children were inside the apartment the whole time. It must be a miracle because things like that don't just happen."

Unexpected Christmas Package

*S*cott and Julianne were sixteen when they met while attending high school in Ann Arbor, Michigan. That day the blonde, blue-eyed teenager was running late for class. When she walked into Scott's homeroom, he pretended to faint and fell off his chair onto the floor.

If Scott's introductory act did not win Julie's heart, it definitely caught her attention. For the next few years until graduation, the two were an item, attending dances together and building a very special kind of friendship.

"One day you'll be wearing my ring, Julie," Scott would tell her. "And then you'll be mine forever."

Julianne would laugh the way only a teenage girl can and bow her head bashfully. "Oh, Scott! That's such a long way off."

But after high school, Scott began commuting by bus to a job at a meatpacking plant some distance from his home and the couple lost track of each other. For two years they neither saw nor heard from each other.

Then, shortly after her twentieth birthday, Julianne was tidying her parents' house when the phone rang.

"I still say you'll wear my ring one day, Julie," the caller said.

"Scott Tschirgi!" She could hardly believe he had called after such a long time. "I thought you forgot about me."

Scott began his courtship by passing by Julie's house each night and serenading her with his harmonica. Julie was thrilled with his renewed interest and almost overnight the relationship between them grew until they knew they could never be apart. A year later, on February 24, Scott made good on his promise and placed a small gold band on Julie's hand in a wedding ceremony attended by dozens of friends and family.

"This isn't the ring I want you to wear," Scott told Julie shortly before the wedding date. "But it will have to do until I can afford to buy you the one you'll wear forever."

Two years later, Julie's mother and her best friend died in a single-car accident. After the funeral, Julie's father tearfully approached Julie and Scott. In his hand was the wedding ring worn by Julie's mother for three decades. "She told me once if anything ever happened to her she wanted you to have it."

Julie took the ring and knew it would always be one of her most prized possessions. A piece of the mother she'd loved and lost.

Later that year, a week before Christmas, Julie and Scott went to a jewelry store in downtown Ann Arbor and had the precious ring engraved. Julie would wear it in place of the smaller ring Scott had bought for their wedding.

"It's the perfect symbol of love," Scott told her as they watched the ring being engraved. "Her love to you, and our love to each other."

The white-gold wedding band was nearly half an inch wide and the jeweler was able to engrave it with their initials and wedding date; the inside of the ring read: JAT-SMT-2-24-68.

"Now and forever this ring will be a reminder to you that I've loved you since the first day I saw you, Julie," Scott told her as he placed it on her finger that afternoon. "And I'll love you till the day I die."

The marriage between Scott and Julie Tschirgi was everything they dreamed it would be. Two years later their son, Mike, was born, followed by a daughter, Dena, and after that another daughter, Tara. The family was close-knit, spending weekends and afternoons camping and fishing the lakes in their area.

Then, one summer, the Tschirgi family went fishing at Half Moon Lake, less than an hour from Ann Arbor. It was a remote lake with a circumference of several miles, and it was a Tschirgi family favorite. The lake was surrounded by a wide rim of rocks that made fishing tricky. Fishermen had to maneuver their way along fifty yards of slippery boulders before reaching the water and casting their lines. But Scott and Julie believed the rocks kept the lake less populated and resulted in a greater catch each time they went. That fall was no exception, and as the day progressed, the Tschirgis began reeling in one succulent catfish after another.

By then Mike was twelve and Tara, the youngest, was seven, and everyone in the family knew how to have fun on a fishing trip. Julie set up a fishing line for the children and helped them catch crawdads from between the rocks.

Finally the sun began to set, and the Tschirgis stopped fishing so they could eat, bundling into warmer clothes because of a chill in the fall air. When the meal was finished, no one wanted to go home; since the fish were biting so well, Scott and Julie agreed to stay longer for some night fishing. They retrieved their lantern from the car and fished until nearly midnight.

Giddy from the long day and the excitement of catching so many catfish and crawdads, the weary Tschirgi family made its way across the rocks toward their car. By then the temperature had dropped even further, and Scott flipped on the car's heater so they could all have a chance to warm up.

Forty minutes later, when they were nearly home, Julianne suddenly gasped out loud.

"My wedding ring!" she cried. "It's gone!"

Scott glanced across the car at his wife's hand and saw that she was right. The place where the ring had been on her finger was now bare.

"We have to go back. I need that ring."

Scott sighed sadly. "It's after one in the morning. The kids are beat and we have to get to bed. I can't go all the way back there tonight."

"Oh, no! I can't believe I lost it. My hand must have gotten cold, and somehow the ring must have fallen off when I was casting out."

Scott was silent a moment. The lake was so vast, the shore so long and covered with hundreds of rocks. Her ring could have fallen between the rocks or been washed out into the lake. There was no way they would ever find it now; he was certain of it.

"We have to go back tomorrow, then," Julie insisted. "Scott, you know what that ring means to me."

Scott nodded. "Yes, I know, honey. But I have to be at work in the morning."

Julie's eyes filled with tears, and her fingers began to shake. "What'll we do?"

"Let's go back next weekend and see if we can find it, all right?"

Reluctantly Julie agreed and waited what seemed like an eternity until the following weekend. First thing Saturday morning, the family piled back into the car and returned to Half Moon Lake to search for the ring.

Although Scott thought he could lead the group to the same spot where they'd fished the previous weekend, the task was more difficult than he'd anticipated. The lake had very few landmarks, and since the rocky shore looked the same all the way around the water, the best he could do was guess at where they had been.

For several hours they hunted for the ring, turning over rocks and running their hands through the shallow water. But the ring was nowhere to be found. Before sundown a defeated Julie walked toward Scott and allowed him to pull her into a hug.

"It's gone, Julie," he said softly. "You have to accept it."

Julie nodded, her chin quivering as she tried to fight back tears. "It meant so much to me, Scott," she said, her voice breaking. "It's the only tangible thing I have to remember Mom by . . . and there'll never be another one like it. I'm so sorry I lost it."

Scott took her in his arms and ran a hand over her back. "You don't need a ring to know how much your mother loved you . . . and you don't need it to know how much I love you, right?"

She dried a trail of tears and nodded. "Right."

"Come on," he said, taking her hand. "Let's go home."

After that Scott bought Julie another ring, but she was still crushed by the loss of her mother's band, and every time they visited the lake she held out a secret hope, a prayer that somehow they'd find it.

As the years passed, Julianne never forgot the ring, often joking that someday someone would catch a fish, cut it open, and find her ring inside.

"I just wish we'd engraved our phone number in it

and not the wedding date," she would say, only partly serious. "That way they could call me when it happens."

But realistically, Julie knew the ring was gone for
good. The seasons affected Half Moon Lake greatly, causing the water to recede thirty feet in some points each
winter and spring before returning to its higher level in
the summer.

Nearly twenty years passed, and eventually Scott retired. He began playing daytime bingo once a week at a
local church hall. Julie was still working but occasionally
she joined him for a game of night bingo. Although their
children had grown and left home to pursue their own
lives, Scott and Julie still went fishing every weekend.

"The thing you'd like about the day crowd at the
bingo hall," Scott would tell Julie, "is that everyone there
is into fishing. That's all we talk about."

In fact, Scott developed a friendship with one couple
in particular. Lisa Chapman worked days at the church
selling bingo cards. Early in their friendship, Scott and
Lisa discovered that Lisa and her husband had fished at
many of the same lakes Scott and Julie had fished. Each
week Scott and Lisa would exchange fishing tales, sharing stories about the biggest catches, the newest hot
spots, and "the one that got away." They learned that
they lived just ten minutes from each other; on several
occasions Lisa and her husband would attend night
bingo and sit alongside Scott and Julie.

On December 22 that year, a day when Scott would
normally have played bingo at the church, he decided

not to go so that he could take care of some last-minute shopping.

"Find me my ring," Julie said, her eyes half teasing, half sad. "Now that would be an amazing Christmas present."

"More like a Christmas miracle." Scott kissed her and smoothed a lock of hair off her forehead. "Go play bingo in my place today. See who caught the most fish over the weekend."

Julie decided the idea was a good one. She had the day off, and since the gifts she'd purchased were wrapped and under the tree, she decided to go. Soon she was in line to purchase bingo cards and was pleased to see that Lisa Chapman was the one selling them.

"Where's your honey?" Lisa asked lightly. "He hasn't missed a Monday bingo session in months."

"Christmas is in three days . . . You know Scott," Julianne said, pulling money from her purse to pay for her bingo cards.

"Well, tell him I caught the biggest catfish of my life last weekend at Half Moon Lake."

Julianne chuckled. "Listen," she said, "if you cut that thing open and find a wedding ring, it's mine. I lost it there twenty-two years ago."

Suddenly Lisa's face went slack and her mouth hung open. "What?" she asked.

"I said, if you find a ring in that fish, it's probably mine. I lost my wedding ring at that lake twenty-two years ago."

"Julie, you're not going to believe this. That fish

didn't have a ring inside it, but fifteen years ago I found a wedding ring at that lake."

"Are you serious?" Julie asked. Her face brightened but fell again just as quickly. "Oh, well," she continued, shrugging off the possibility, "there's no way it's my ring. It's been gone too long. I'm sure it's at the bottom of the lake by now."

"Wait, describe your ring."

Julie looked strangely at Lisa. "It was a wide band, white gold with etchings on the top and bottom. And it was engraved."

"Oh, my word, Julie, you aren't going to believe this! I have that ring!"

Quickly Lisa recounted how she had found it.

Fifteen years earlier, Lisa and her husband, Jim, had made an annual springtime trek to Half Moon Lake to search the shores for fishing lures. The lake typically receded so far that the rocks no longer lined the shore, and the people were able to climb past the rocks and walk along the sandy shoreline. That afternoon Lisa and Jim found very few usable lures, but they did find a wedding ring lying partially buried in the sand.

"Look at this," Lisa said to her husband that afternoon.

Jim made his way toward his wife and examined the ring and its engraved markings on the inside. "A wedding ring," he said. "I'll bet someone's been missing it."

Lisa then examined the ring once more and placed it in her pocket.

"What are you going to do with it?" Jim asked.

"I don't know for sure, but it's obviously a nice ring. I can't just leave it here on the beach."

When they returned home, Lisa thought through her options. She could place an ad in the newspaper that covered Half Moon Lake area. But then people from hundreds of miles away fished at the lake, and there was no telling if the person who lost it would ever see the newspaper. She was also hesitant because of the date on the ring—February 24, 1968. If someone had lost the ring in the 1960s, they would certainly have stopped looking for it by now. In the end, Lisa decided her only option was to put it aside.

"I know I'll never find the owner of that ring," she told her husband. "But it meant something to someone, and I can't just throw it out."

88

She placed it in a jar with other odds and ends and never thought about it again until Julie Tschirgi stood in front of her that June afternoon at the bingo hall.

"Wait a minute," Lisa said as a dozen people in line listened to the exchange between the two women. Lisa summoned another worker to the table to take her place. "I'll be right back. I'm going home to get that ring."

Fifteen minutes later, Lisa returned to the bingo hall with a large white gold wedding band on her finger. She walked up to Julie, who was sitting near a group of people who had heard the women talking about the ring. Julie and the others were now waiting anxiously to see if it was indeed the missing ring.

At home Lisa had checked the initials on the ring and knew instantly that it was Julie's missing wedding band. Grinning wildly, she approached Julie and held up her hand.

"Looky here," she said.

Julie was shocked. She stood slowly and moved toward Lisa, never taking her eyes from the ring. It was the very ring her mother had worn, the one she and Scott had taken in to be engraved, the one she'd prayed to find every day since losing it nearly two decades earlier. She would have known the ring from across the bingo hall, but she reached out and removed it from Lisa's hand, turning it over in her own.

"It's my ring," she said finally, tears falling onto her cheeks. "We got it engraved at Christmas, and now I'm getting it back at Christmas. I can't believe it."

As she said the words, the people around her broke into a loud round of applause. Several of them had glistening eyes themselves at the sight of Julie's happy tears.

"Is this unbelievable or what?" Lisa said. "You lost the ring all those years ago, I find it years after that, and now fifteen years after that, we play bingo together, and all this time I've had your ring sitting in a jar in my house."

At that moment the pastor of the church heard the commotion and approached them. He listened to the story behind the ring, and then Julie asked him if he would bless it.

"Mrs. Tschirgi, I don't believe that's necessary," the pastor said. "If the good Lord helped you find that ring after all these years—at Christmastime no less—I'd say that ring has already been blessed."

Again the crowd erupted into applause, and Lisa and Julie embraced.

"Thank you doesn't seem like enough," Julie said, laughing through her tears. "I've never forgotten this ring, even after all these years. And now it's mine again."

Later Scott and Julie considered the odds against what had happened. The lake was almost an hour away from their home. It was absurd to imagine that a neighbor would visit the same lake where she'd lost her ring and find it there after years of high and low tides. Not to mention that they would then befriend that neighbor and that one day Julie would mention the missing ring in front of her.

"Even if that lake was completely dry and we searched up and down the length of it every day for an entire summer, we very well might never have found that ring," Scott told his wife as they wondered over the wedding band once more. "It should have been several feet under sand after all that time."

"But it wasn't. And now it's mine once more."

The couple was silent for a moment. "Scott, do you believe in miracles?" Julie asked him.

"Of course," he said as he pulled Julie close. "I told you that ring was a sign of very strong love . . . your mother's and ours. Now it's found its way back. Merry Christmas, honey."

Christmas Angels

*A*ustin Rozelle was four years old when his parents noticed his imagination truly taking wing. He loved sports, particularly basketball, and often pretended to be the greatest player of all, Michael Jordan. At bedtime when the Rozelles' children asked for favorite bedtime stories, Austin's request never changed.

"Tell me a Michael Jordan story, Daddy, please!"

And Burt Rozelle would make up a story involving Austin and Michael Jordan and some type of crucial basketball game. It got so that as Christmas approached that year, Austin wanted only one thing: a visit from Michael Jordan. Throughout the month of December, whenever the doorbell would ring at the Rozelle house, Austin would run toward the front door yelling, "It's probably Michael Jordan!"

So it was that three days before Christmas, when Austin dribbled his child-sized basketball into the family's Portland, Oregon, house and announced he was going to Michael's house, his mother thought nothing of it. Austin was always pretending to be visiting with Michael Jordan or taking a trip to his house.

That Sunday afternoon the air was particularly damp, and Austin tugged on his mother's skirt while she washed the dishes. "Bye, Mom. I'm going to see Michael Jordan."

Stella Rozelle smiled at the child. "Okay, Austin, have fun."

Obviously Austin had no idea where Michael Jordan lived, nor that he did not even live in Oregon. Even if he had known the exact location, Stella knew the boy would never really leave the house. Especially by himself.

Austin was merely playing a game of make-believe, as he had so many other times, and Stella felt at ease as she continued her conversation and watched the child disappear into the backyard.

Fifteen minutes later, Stella finished the dishes and sauntered outside to round up Austin and his six-year-old brother, Daniel. The older child was swinging on the family swingset, happily humming a tune from Sunday school earlier that day. The temperature was dropping, and Stella wanted the children to come inside before they caught cold.

"It's getting too cold out here, buddy. Let's go inside

and have some dinner." She glanced around the yard. "Where's Austin?"

Daniel shrugged as he jumped off the swing. "He was dribbling his ball and he went out that way." Daniel pointed down the street. "He told me he was going to see Michael Jordan."

Suddenly Stella's blood ran cold as she remembered a billboard she'd forgotten until now. It was two miles away on Martin Luther King Boulevard, and it had a larger-than-life photograph of Michael Jordan. "Daniel, you don't think he's going to that billboard picture of Michael Jordan, do you?"

Daniel thought for a moment and then shrugged. "Probably. He told me once that he thinks Michael lives there."

Stella's heart was immediately in her throat. She ran into the house, found Burt in the computer room, and explained the situation.

"You can't find him anywhere?" Burt's face immediately drained of all its color.

She felt panic welling within her, and she shook her head. "He's gone, Burt. Pray. Please pray."

Stella called a neighbor to come stay with Daniel, and she and Burt searched the house and yard again.

"What's the last thing you remember him saying or doing?" Burt asked as they climbed into the car and set off slowly down the street, straining to see into every yard.

Stella ran her fingers nervously through her hair. "I was doing dishes, getting ready for dinner, when Austin came in with his ball and told me he was going to see Michael Jordan."

"He says that all the time."

"Exactly. I thought he was just playing and I said okay."

Burt rounded the corner as the two of them exchanged a terrified look. Thirty minutes had passed since Austin's disappearance. If their son had attempted the two-mile walk to Martin Luther King Boulevard by himself, he could have been kidnapped or hit by a car. In addition, the weather had forecasted snow and Austin wasn't dressed warmly enough for the near-freezing temperatures. Most frightening of all, he could be anywhere because the child was too young to have any sense of direction.

While Burt wove their car up and down the side streets leading toward the busy thoroughfare, Stella used their cell phone to call the police. "Our little boy wandered off and we can't find him anywhere. We think he might be trying to get to MLK Boulevard."

"What's your child look like?" the officer asked.

"He's four years old, about three and a half feet tall, white-blond hair, dimples, and blue eyes. He's wearing a black and red sweat suit with white tennis shoes and a Chicago Bulls baseball cap. He was dribbling a basketball when he left."

Burt continued to drive the streets near their house, and Stella searched up and down each sidewalk as she waited for the police officer to take a full report. Every moment that passed meant that Austin could be getting picked up by a stranger or run over. She struggled to breathe, suffocated by the feeling of helplessness. Would they be forced to celebrate Christmas without finding Austin? Would they be making funeral plans?

On the verge of hysteria, she covered her face with her hands and began to pray. Suddenly the story of baby Jesus came to mind—the ways in which King Herod tried to have the Christ child killed. At every turn angels were there to protect Jesus. "Please, God . . ." she prayed out loud. "Please watch over Austin and lead me to him. Put your Christmas angels around him, wherever he is."

Burt and Stella were deeply faithful Christians and had been all their lives. Together they had taught their boys to pray and trust God in any situation where they felt they needed help. But a few months before, Stella's mother had died of a brain tumor, and since then she had felt none of the joy that usually accompanied her faith. She had even tried letting go of her sorrow by counting her blessings, but she was still left feeling sad and empty.

Now, as she sat helplessly in the passenger seat, praying they would find Austin, she was keenly aware of how precious life was and how desperately she wanted to find her son and hold him close again. They circled the block surrounding her house and branched out onto Martin Luther King Boulevard, but there was no sign of Austin.

"Put your angels around him, God . . . ," she whispered again. "Please take care of him and lead us to him."

Suddenly the cloud of sorrow lifted and she knew how very blessed she was, the mother of two beautiful children, married to a loving, faithful man who cherished her and the children. If only she could find Austin, Stella knew she would never take these—God's greatest blessings—for granted again.

They continued to search intently along dozens of streets, but when fifteen minutes passed, they returned home for an update. The police were there, talking with the neighbor, when they pulled in.

"Any sign of him?" The officer looked troubled, as though he knew something terrible had happened.

"Nothing." Burt was already headed back for the car. "We'll trace the route again. He's gotta be somewhere."

The officer agreed to look in the opposite direction, and the two men made plans to meet back at the house in twenty minutes for an update.

96

Burt hung his head and began crying as he started the car engine. "Not Austin," he shouted through his tears. "Not my Austin!"

"Pray, Burt," Stella implored as she craned her neck, trying to see up and down sidewalks they'd already checked twice. "Please pray."

The couple set out again, working their way out from the Rozelle house in every possible direction. As they drove, they prayed aloud.

"Please lead us to him, and please, God, please protect him. Send your Christmas angels like you did two thousand years ago for baby Jesus . . ." Stella's tears streamed down her face. "Please, God," she added, her voice barely a whisper. "He's only four years old."

Terrible thoughts filled their heads as they continued to search: Austin lying in a gutter covered with blood, or miles away in the car of some evil stranger. Stella knew that wherever he was, the child was scared and probably crying for her and Burt. The thought made the search unbearable, yet the pair had no choice but to continue.

Nearly an hour after the boy had disappeared and more than a mile from their house, they turned onto a busy street one block from Martin Luther King Boulevard and saw a foursome on the sidewalk half a block ahead. Two tall, slim, dark-haired women and a younger, blonde woman were walking together a few feet behind a boy with blond hair wearing a red and black sweatshirt and black sweatpants. The child was carrying a basketball.

"Austin!" Burt shouted. He sped up, pulling alongside the three women and little Austin and quickly parking the car. "Austin! Thank you, God. Thank you."

"Austin!" Stella shouted as she jumped out of the car and joined them. The women stood back and watched as Stella and Burt swept the little boy into their arms. Relieved and sobbing, Stella fell to her knees next to Austin and pulled him tightly to her, stroking his hair and closing her eyes.

"We thought we'd lost you, baby," she cried into his downy soft hair. "Thank you, God."

"I wasn't lost, Mommy. I was going to Michael Jordan's house!" Austin smiled easily, calm and unaffected by his adventure away from home.

Standing back, careful not to interrupt the reunion, the women who had been trailing behind the boy smiled.

"He's a character, that one," the older woman said

softly. "He was chasing his ball and he fell into a ditch back there a ways. There was a bit of water in it and we helped him out. We've been following him ever since so he wouldn't get hurt."

Stella nodded, still clinging tightly to the child. "Thank you so much," she said, wiping at her tears and looking Austin over to be sure he was all right.

The woman continued. "He said he was going to Michael Jordan's house."

The other tall woman smiled. "Isn't he that professional basketball player?"

"Yes." Stella couldn't take her eyes from Austin, relieved and grateful beyond words that her son was unharmed.

"Does he live around here?" The older woman wrinkled her nose, clearly confused.

Burt shook his head and uttered a short laugh as he tousled Austin's hair. "Austin has quite an imagination lately." He looked at Stella. "I guess we didn't know exactly how much."

"Anyway," the woman said, "he seemed to know where he was going."

Stella nodded, paying little attention to the women. She swept the boy into her arms and thanked the women once more for their help. Then, fresh tears of relief streaming down her cheeks, she and Burt drove off to share the good news with the police and the others.

They were at the end of the street when Burt hit the brakes. "How thoughtless of me—I should have offered those women a ride home. It's freezing outside."

He did a U-turn and headed back down the block, but the women were gone. Stella checked her watch. Not even two minutes had passed since they had left the women, but now as she and Burt looked up the street, there was no one in sight.

"That's strange," she muttered aloud. "No one could walk that fast. I wonder where they went."

"Let's keep looking," Burt said. "Maybe if we drive the length of the street we'll find them resting somewhere."

For ten minutes Burt and Stella drove back and forth on the street looking carefully for the women who had so kindly watched over Austin.

"You're right," Stella said. "I feel awful. They were so nice to look after Austin and then we didn't even offer them a ride home."

"Oh, well," Burt finally said. "I guess they got home some other way."

There was silence for a moment as Stella thought about her prayer. *Protect him with your Christmas angels . . .*

"Burt," Stella said, her voice quieter than before. "You don't think they might have been angels, do you?"

"Oh, Stella, come on. They were just friendly women taking a walk and doing a kind deed."

"You're right," Stella said. She thought about Austin falling into the ditch and remembered how a man in nearby Vancouver had fallen into a similar bog once and been trapped by the mud. He'd nearly died of hypothermia before rescuers found him. She shuddered. A child would never have fared so well. "Well, whoever they were, they were an answer to our prayers, that's for sure."

Back at the house, Stella and Burt ran inside with Austin in their arms. "We found him walking a mile from here. Three neighborhood women were walking behind him, watching out for him."

"Oh, thank you, dear Lord." The neighbor kissed Austin on the cheek and then left the Rozelles to themselves. By then Daniel had come into the room, awed by the fact that Austin had actually left and grateful that he was home safe. Burt and Stella put their arms around Austin, pulling him close once more as the family formed a circle.

"We were worried about you, Austin," Stella said softly.

"I know, Mommy. I won't go to Michael Jordan's house anymore. Next time he'll come here."

"That's good," Burt said.

Stella smiled and took the boy's cold damp hands in hers. "Listen, Austin, remember those ladies who helped you and stayed with you?"

The child nodded. "Yes, Mommy. They were strangers."

"But you weren't afraid of them, were you?"

"No, they were nice."

Burt nodded. "Yes, they looked after you. Did they tell you their names?"

"They told me they were from God," Austin said simply.

There was a pause as Stella, Burt, and Daniel leaned closer, curious expressions on their faces.

"Oh, yeah." Austin looked up at his mother. "What's an angel, Mommy?"

The adults stared at the child for a moment, and then exchanged a knowing look as goose bumps rose up on each of their arms. Quietly, and with a greater understanding than at any time in his life, Burt directed his family to hold hands; then he closed his eyes and bowed his head. When he spoke, his voice was filled with awe.

"Dear God, we do not know your ways and we do not pretend to have answers. But somehow today we know that you brought about divine intervention in the life of our little Austin. Thank you for hearing our prayers and bringing him home safely. And, God—" Burt paused, his voice choked with emotion. "Thank you for the simple faith of our children. And thank you for your Christmas angels."

The Holy
Hand of God

*I*t was Christmas, and the Kramer family had shared a wonderful holiday together at their home in central New Mexico. In addition to their presents, the family felt thankful for things that could not be wrapped and placed under a tree. Brian was very happy in his job as a local resort manager, and Ann was four months pregnant with their third child. Their first two, Kari, five, and Kiley, four, were healthy and happy and the source of much joy. In fact, the Kramer family couldn't have been happier.

After celebrating Christmas at home that year, the family climbed into their Chevy Suburban and headed for a small town about twenty minutes north of Santa Fe. Since Brian's parents lived in Santa Fe, he knew the roads well and enjoyed the scenic drive.

"It never gets old, does it?" Brian asked his wife, reaching over to hold her hand as they climbed the mountains outside of Santa Fe. "God sure knows how to make things beautiful."

Ann smiled and placed his hand on her pregnant abdomen. "He sure does."

The visit with Brian's parents was fun filled and full of the laughter of Kari and Kiley, but after two days it was time to return home. A light snow was falling as they packed up the Suburban and said their good-byes.

"I hate to drive in snow," Ann said as they climbed in and buckled their seat belts.

"I know," Brian said calmly. "But you're not driving. I am. And I'm perfectly fine with it. Just say a prayer that we get home safely."

Ann nodded and silently asked God to guard their car as they drove home. That done, she did her best not to worry. She stared out her window and admitted that the snow was certainly beautiful. It fell gently and looked like freshly sifted powdered sugar on the ground.

The highway that led from Santa Fe toward the Kramers' home was a two-lane road with an occasional passing lane. From Brian's parents' house the highway climbed slightly until it reached two small towns, and then it continued downhill for nearly forty minutes before leveling out in the valley.

Although traffic was light that morning, Brian drove

slowly and carefully, aware that there were patches of ice under the snow-covered road. Most of the cars on the road had snow chains on their tires, and though the Kramers' did not, they felt secure in their Surburban with four-wheel drive and heavy-duty snow tires.

Still, Brian sensed his wife's fears as they began the section of highway that was nearly straight downhill. He glanced at his wife and smiled warmly. "Honey, it'll be okay. Don't worry."

"I know, I know," Ann said. "I just wish we were home, that's all."

"We'll be home soon. Try to relax."

Ann nodded, but she could feel a tension throughout her body. The road seemed especially slippery, despite the fact that Brian was driving in a low gear.

104

Just as the highway became steep, Brian shifted into yet a lower gear just to be sure they wouldn't lose traction. Suddenly the back of the Suburban began fishtailing across the road, swinging from one side of the highway to the other. Brian struggled to correct the truck's steering, but as he turned the wheel, he could feel that it was having no effect on the tires. Suddenly he knew what had happened. The vehicle was in a slide with the tires completely detached from the road.

At that instant the Suburban swung sharply toward oncoming traffic, sending the vehicle spinning in a complete circle.

"Oh, God!" Ann screamed, grabbing on to the dashboard. "In the name of God, please stop!"

The Suburban stopped spinning and began a fast

sideways slide toward the cliff that buttressed the edge of the highway. If the vehicle slid off the road, Brian and Ann knew they would probably be killed since the fall would send them several hundred feet down the hill along rough terrain.

"God, please help us!" Ann screamed again. But deep in her heart she knew they were traveling far too fast, and she felt certain that they were going over the edge.

Then, just before the drop-off, the Suburban slammed to a sudden stop. Kiley had taken off her seat belt, and the harsh jolt sent the child flying across the car into the window.

For a moment there was silence.

Brian looked at his wife in shock, not believing that they had avoided going over the edge of the highway. He was amazed that they were alive.

"Girls, are you okay?" he asked, turning around.

"Yes, Daddy," came a small voice. "I hit my head, but I'm okay."

Relieved, Brian stared at his wife once more. "We must have hit a tree stump or a boulder or something," he said.

"Maybe a guardrail," Ann added.

Still shaky from the closeness of what could have been a deadly car accident, Brian climbed out of the vehicle. He walked around it to the front. There was nothing in between the Suburban and the sheer drop.

"Ann, come here!" Brian said loudly. "Come see this!" Ann opened her door and slid carefully onto the small space between the vehicle and the side of the cliff. "What did we hit?" she asked.

"That's just it. We didn't hit anything. There's not a rock or a piece of wood, no guardrail. Nothing. The truck just stopped for no reason at all."

Ann examined the edge of the road and saw that Brian was right. The vehicle had been sliding at more than ten miles per hour and had suddenly stopped for no explainable reason. Together they looked down the jagged, rocky mountainside and shuddered at the thought of what might have happened.

"Ann, it's like the hand of God just reached out and stopped us from going over the mountainside."

Quietly Ann remembered her desperate plea for God to help them. She reached over and circled her arms around her husband's waist, resting her head on his chest. "With all my heart I believe you're right. We were stopped by the hand of God. It must have been a miracle. A Christmas miracle."

His Mysterious Ways

*B*ack then there was no way for anyone in the Cannucci family to know how special that summer of 1939 would become. It started out like any other and would have been uneventful for the Cannucci children if it weren't for Maria Fiona. While their mother tended to household duties, eleven-year-old Sara Cannucci was put in charge of keeping her little brother, Tony, occupied.

One morning soon after summer started, Sara was playing with Tony outside the house in New Jersey, where their family rented the upstairs, when Maria walked past with a bag of groceries. Maria and her husband had no children yet, but that morning Sara noticed that Maria was pregnant.

"Hey," she called out. "Want some help?"

Maria stopped and smiled at the young girl. She had married into the Fiona family, and not long after they had decided to turn the upstairs floor of their trilevel house into an apartment, the Cannucci family had become their tenants. Not until after the families had shared the house for several months did they realize that their ancestors had lived in the same Sicilian village in Italy many years earlier.

"I don't believe in coincidence," the senior Cannucci would tell his children. "Our families were together back then and we're together now. There must be a reason for that."

Now, as Maria looked at the young Cannucci children, she welcomed their help. After all, they were practically family.

"Sure, Sara, I'd love the help." Maria set down her bag and watched Sara take her brother's hand and scramble to pick up the bag. The children trailed behind as Maria entered her apartment.

"Why don't you set them there," Maria said, pointing to a small kitchen table. Then she looked at the blond-haired boy peeking out from behind his big sister's skirt.

"Well, hi there, Tony," she said. Looking at Sara, she smiled warmly. "Would you two like to stay for some cookies and maybe I could bring out some paper and colorful pencils?"

Sara was thrilled with the idea, and for the rest of the

morning the children stayed at the Fiona house visiting with Maria. Just before they left to go home, Tony walked up to Maria and stared at her protruding stomach. Maria smiled and tentatively Tony reached up, touching her gently with his pudgy hand.

"Ball?" he asked.

Maria laughed and her cheeks grew red. "No, it's not a ball. It's a baby. I have a baby inside my tummy."

The child's eyes grew wide. "Baby? Inside you?" he asked.

"Yes." Maria held his hand and moved it over her taut midsection. "It's okay to touch it. Maybe you'll feel my baby kicking."

Tony left his hand on Maria and continued to stare at her abdomen. "Love baby," he said softly. "My baby."

Maria smiled again. "No, sweetie. It's my baby. But when it's born you can be his or her friend. Okay?"

Tony seemed satisfied with the answer and nodded. Then he leaned over and kissed Maria's stomach before skipping away with his sister.

After that, the children returned every morning, and Maria was happy to have the company. Her husband was a shoemaker, and she was often lonely while he kept long hours at the shop. She enjoyed visiting with the Cannucci children and was especially taken by Tony. Each time the boy visited, he was enthralled with Maria's pregnant body. He would pat Maria's stomach and stare at her, even resting his head on her. Sometimes the child would feel the baby kick and he would squeal in delight.

"I don't understand it," Sara said, looking strangely

at her brother. "Tony has been around other pregnant mothers. We know many pregnant women, even now, and he never made this sort of fuss over her."

"Maybe they're going to be special friends," Maria said, patting Tony's golden hair as he laid his head on her stomach.

Tony talked constantly about holding the baby, even though he did not understand how the infant was going to come out of Maria's stomach. Then one day Maria went to the hospital, and four days later she returned home with a tiny wrapped bundle in her arms.

"His name is Sal," Maria said, stooping low so that Tony could see the baby.

The older child was enthralled by the baby's tiny hands and feet and the miniature face. "My baby?" he asked Maria once again.

110

"Your friend, Tony. Baby Sal is your friend."

Sara smiled as she watched the exchange and wondered what would happen as the years passed, whether Baby Sal and Tony really would become friends.

But only two months later, the Cannucci family moved away to be closer to the butcher shop where Tony Senior worked. For weeks afterward, Tony spoke of Baby Sal and seemed sad that he had moved. But as winter arrived, the child discovered other things that captured his attention and he forgot about the tiny baby. And the years passed.

Two years after Tony graduated from high school, he enlisted in the Army and was sent to Panama for two years. There he and his fellow soldiers were exposed to the systemic herbicide Agent Orange, which the Army used as a defoliant in areas where troops were stationed. Oftentimes Tony and the other young men in his division would get violently ill and have to spend days in the infirmary. But never was a connection made between the harsh chemical herbicide and their sickness.

In 1958, at age twenty-two, Tony returned to Albany and reestablished himself as a student at New Jersey State University. He soon earned his teaching credentials and began working in the same neighborhood where he'd grown up. Eventually he married, had two beautiful children, and gave up teaching for a better salary working with the New Jersey State Labor Department as a training director.

At about the same time, early in 1970, Tony began feeling ill and losing weight. Several weeks after he first began having symptoms, a doctor confirmed his worst fears. He had hairy cell leukemia, a rare form of lymphoma that was both painful and deadly.

111

"Sara, please pray for me," Tony asked his sister when he told her the news. "I'm not ready to die yet."

"Ah, Tony." Sara could hardly believe that her younger brother had cancer. "Of course I'll pray. I'll pray for a miracle."

For nearly a decade Tony was in and out of remission, but then he began worsening. His spleen was surgically removed, and after the operation the doctor told him he probably did not have long to live.

Determined to beat the odds, Tony changed doctors and in 1979 began seeing a specialist in the field of hematology, Dr. Taylor Johnson, at a hospital in New Jersey.

"The other doctor wrote me off," Tony told Dr. Johnson. "Now don't you go and do that, okay? I've got a lot more living to do."

Dr. Johnson smiled. "You're very sick, Tony," he said. "But I think we can help you here. Besides, I want you to be around for the big test."

"The big test?"

"Yes, Tony. Interferon. It's an experimental drug right now, but it might be just what you need."

"Well, let's get it going."

Dr. Johnson shook his head. "Not yet. It'll take a few years before it'll be ready. My job will be to keep you around until then."

Tony's outlook was very positive and his condition improved, but more than a year later in 1980, Dr. Johnson phoned him to say he was retiring from his practice.

"But don't worry. I've got a brilliant young doctor taking my place. If anyone can keep you alive until the Interferon is available, it's Dr. Fiona."

"Dr. Fiona?" Tony was puzzled. "That name sounds familiar."

"Well, I think you both grew up in New Jersey, so you've probably heard his name somewhere. I've set up an appointment for you to meet him right away."

The first meeting between Tony and the young doctor was upbeat and positive.

"Your condition is serious," Dr. Fiona said. "But I

think I can help you stay alive until the Interferon is ready."

Dr. Fiona was tireless, spending hours with Tony testing his blood and advising him about his condition. Throughout that year and the next, there were several times when Tony nearly died. He would lie on a hospital bed clinging to life while machines cleaned his blood. Almost always Dr. Fiona would sit beside him holding his hand and praying for him. For Dr. Fiona, Tony was more than a patient with a rare form of leukemia. The two had grown up in Albany and had ancestors who were originally from Italy. Because of that, Dr. Fiona cared deeply for Tony and devoted himself to helping the man and his family deal with his cancer.

113

"Sometimes, all we can do is ask God to take over," he would say occasionally. "We're doing all we can, and now it's up to him."

Despite his brushes with death, Tony lived, and Dr. Fiona continued to help him fight for time. Then, in the late 1980s, when Interferon finally became available, Dr. Fiona made sure that Tony was one of the first leukemia patients to use it. Almost immediately Tony's body grew stronger, and by late 1989 he was in remission.

"You saved my life, Doc," Tony said to him when he got the news. "I'm supposed to be dead right now, but you never gave up."

"We did it together, Tony. You, me, and God. You've always been special to me. You're a fighter." He paused a moment. "And now I have something you can really fight for."

Tony listened as Dr. Fiona explained that he wanted Tony to help him with a Christmas telethon he was about to do to raise awareness about leukemia and possible chemical causes. He also wanted to work with Tony in filing suit against the U.S. Army for exposing Tony to Agent Orange.

"I'm sure that Agent Orange is what caused your leukemia," Dr. Fiona said. Both men knew that by then Agent Orange had been partially banned because of its harmful side effects. "Now we need to see that nothing like that ever happens again to a group of soldiers." He paused. "I know it'll take up some of your Christmas time . . . but you know how God works. You're bound to get more than you give."

Dr. Fiona's zeal was contagious, and Tony agreed heartily to help in the fight against both leukemia and government-approved exposure to harmful chemicals. The Christmas telethon was set to take place in a month, and since Tony would be on television, his sister, Sara, working as a reporter in New Milford, Connecticut, promised to watch.

"Wave to me," she told Tony.

Tony laughed. "Oh, sure, Sara, you bet."

Then there was silence for a moment, and when Sara spoke, her voice was serious. "Really, Tony. I'm so glad you're okay. I'm proud of you for being such a fighter."

"It wasn't me, it was Dr. Fiona."

"Dr. Fiona?"

"You know, the doctor who's been helping me these past ten years."

"I know, I know. I've met him a dozen times when you were in the hospital. It's just that his name sounds so familiar."

"I thought so, too. He grew up in Albany, so we probably went to the same schools or something. Who knows?"

Now, on Christmas day, as Sara tuned in the station carrying the telethon, she was still puzzled by the name of Tony's doctor. Where had she heard the name Fiona before?

She watched the telethon intently and saw that Tony was looking very well. He had survived hairy cell leukemia for nearly twenty years, and because of Dr. Fiona's tireless monitoring and testing and his cancer-fighting procedures, Tony was the longest-living survivor of that form of cancer.

115

Sara watched as the cameras showed Dr. Fiona standing beside Tony, and suddenly she had a flashback. In her mind she pictured her brother as a three-year-old towhead nuzzling his face against the pregnant abdomen of Maria Fiona.

"My God, could it be?" she wondered out loud. The Fiona family had rented a flat to the Cannucci family when Sara was a young girl. Maria was pregnant back then, and Tony would have been about three years old.

That night Sara called her brother excitedly.

"Tony, do you know your doctor's mother's name?" she asked.

Tony was puzzled at her interest. "Sure," he said. "Maria."

Sara was stunned. "I don't believe it," she said. "I just don't believe it."

She was flooded by a sudden wave of memories.

"What is it, Sara?"

"Do you remember when we lived on North Eighteenth Street? You were just a little boy."

Tony thought a moment. "Not really. I've heard about it. An apartment or something we rented from another family."

"Tony, we rented from the Fiona family. You and I used to go and visit Maria Fiona, and you would always touch her stomach when she was pregnant. You were in awe over her unborn child, always looking at her and patting her and trying to feel the baby kick."

"Okay, so?" Tony still did not see the connection.

"Don't you understand? That baby was Sal Fiona. Your doctor. The one who saved your life. You were so taken by the life of that unborn child, and then that child grew up and saved yours."

"Are you serious?"

"Yes. I prayed for a miracle, Tony," Sara said confidently. "And God was working one all along."

Tony was stunned at the thought, and within minutes was on the telephone with Dr. Fiona.

"Yes, when I was born we were living on North Eighteenth Street," Dr. Fiona said.

For a while the two men said nothing, absorbed in the realization of how their pasts had connected.

"It's just about impossible to imagine something like that happening," Tony said finally.

Sal Fiona smiled at his end of the conversation. "Not really, Tony. You might have been only a child, but children are always closer to God." The doctor paused. "I told you God would give you something back for your time on Christmas day."

Christmas Roses

Tara had nothing else to do that winter day, so when her friend saw her at school and asked her to come over for dinner, she shrugged and readily agreed.

"My brother's having the football team over," her friend explained. "If you come, at least I won't be the only girl."

Tara laughed, and after talking with her friend a while longer, made plans to see her that evening. Although Tara did not follow football, she knew that her friend's brother was on a semiprofessional team based in Tulsa, Oklahoma. She was intrigued and made sure to do her hair carefully before walking to her friend's house down the street.

That evening as the house filled with nearly thirty football players, Tara felt herself growing shy. She had just turned twenty and had always been quiet around boys, especially when they were in large groups as they were that night. After a while she separated herself and sat by the fireplace to warm her feet. While she was there, a handsome football player came over and introduced himself.

"I'm Andrew Mastalli." The young man grinned, his eyes sparkling in the light of the fire. "But everyone calls me Andy."

Tara couldn't help but laugh, and with the ice broken the two talked through much of the evening. Andy was twenty years old too and determined to play football as long as possible. Tara listened intently as Andy spoke of his dreams, and when the evening ended, since Tara lived just three blocks away, Andy offered to walk her home.

"Know what I don't like about the winter?" Andy asked as they made their way to Tara's house.

"What?"

"No roses."

"Roses?" Tara asked curiously.

"Roses are the best. Someday I want a home with my very own rosebush. There's nothing like the smell of roses in the summertime."

Tara smiled at her interesting companion. The next day when he called to take her for a drive, she wasn't surprised.

"There's an attraction there," Tara told her friend a

few weeks later, after she and Andy had dated several times. "But neither of us wants to get serious right now."

Since neither of their families had much money and Andy's mother was ill, the couple waited eight years before getting married. When they did, Andy brought Tara a rose to carry down the aisle.

"Now nothing can separate us, Tara," he told her. "This is the happiest day of my life."

Although a knee injury ended his football career, throughout the next twenty-eight years Andy and Tara shared a relationship few people ever have. Andy even got his wish—not long after they were married, they planted a rosebush in the yard of their home in Tulsa.

Then, shortly after his fifty-fourth birthday, Andy was passed over for a promotion at the school where he was the head maintenance worker.

"The kids loved him, the faculty loved him, everyone loved him," Tara told her close friend sometime later. "The administrator was the only one who had something against him."

When it became clear that Andy wouldn't be getting the promotion, he began suffering symptoms of stress. He had headaches and chest pains and complained about feeling tired. Tara was worried about him and arranged for him to see a doctor.

"You need to take it easy, Mr. Mastalli," the doctor told him. "But I don't think there's anything seriously wrong with you."

But on a sunny afternoon just one week after the appointment with the doctor, Andy suffered a massive heart attack. Tara rushed to the hospital to be by Andy's side, but there was nothing the doctors could do. Andy died.

The love of Tara's life was gone forever. Without Andy, she plummeted into a deep depression that nothing could ease.

For weeks after his death, students sent letters to Tara telling her what a wonderful man Andy had been and stating how badly they missed him. But nothing helped Tara's grief.

Over the next several months Tara lost weight and rarely left the home she and Andy had shared. It was not until late that year that she began seeing friends and spending more time socializing. She even went on a few casual outings with a male friend of hers. But her heartbreak over losing Andy was still so great that it hurt too much to go out with the man. Christmas was approaching—Andy's favorite time of the year—and she could not stop the terrible ache inside at missing him.

121

"I don't know when I can see you again," she told her male friend one night. I still have so much of my past to deal with. You see, Andy and I were married for nearly thirty years. I just don't know how to stop loving him after all that time."

The week leading up to Christmas was perhaps the darkest of all for Tara, who felt as if she'd made an attempt to live again and failed. She still missed Andy so badly that she thought she might never leave home again.

Christmas morning dawned, and Tara awoke to the heavy smell of . . . roses. Puzzled, Tara climbed out of bed and wandered through the house. There was a Christmas snow on the ground, and outside everything around her was frozen. Still, as she made her way from one room to the next, she was overwhelmed by the smell of Andy's favorite flower.

Quickly she went to the telephone and dialed her friend and neighbor, Lisa.

"Please, Lisa. Come over right away," she asked her friend. "I know it's Christmas morning, but I have to see you. Just for a minute." She did not mention the roses because she wanted to see if the smell was only in her imagination. Since it was so strong, she knew that if she wasn't imagining it, Lisa would recognize it as soon as she walked into the house.

"Hey, where are the roses?" Lisa asked as she opened the door bundled in a coat and boots. "It's Christmas. No one's supposed to have roses."

Tara stared at her friend strangely, and tears filled her eyes. Lisa realized that something was wrong. "What is it, Tara?"

"There aren't any roses in the house. None at all. And there can't be any on the bush outside because it's frozen solid."

Lisa looked around, and suddenly an expression of understanding filled her face.

"It's from God, Tara," she said. "He must want you to know that Andy's fine and that everything's going to be okay. You can go on with your life."

"Do you really think so?" Tara asked, sitting down and steadying herself in the chair.

"Yes. How else can you explain this smell? It's so strong it can't be anything else."

Tara nodded slowly. "You're right." Then she began to cry softly. How good God was, letting Tara know that he still cared—that somewhere Andy still waited for her. It was the greatest Christmas present Tara could ever have received, and with it came a sense of peace and closure.

"I guess it's time for me to let go."

At that instant the smell of fresh roses disappeared from the room. Tara looked at Lisa to see if she had noticed.

"It's gone," Lisa said simply.

"Yes. As soon as I said it was time to let go."

Tara has never again smelled roses in the dead of winter as she did that cold Christmas day. Soon after that, she began socializing with her friends again, and in time her depression disappeared completely. Although she has male friends, she has never remarried.

"There will never be anyone like Andy again," she told Lisa some time later.

As if to remind herself of that fact, she has kept a rosebush every year without fail. Each summer when the flowers bloom, she is taken back to that Christmas day when she was not sure whether she could live without the man she had loved for so long. And Tara remembers the smell of roses and how by some miracle God himself gave her the strength to go on.

Heavenly Hindrances

*P*astor George W. Nubert looked at his watch and took a deep breath. His wife was busy making dinner in the kitchen, and he had ten minutes to get over to the church, light the coal furnace, and be back in time for dinner. Sometimes he felt like he was performing a circus act, twirling plates in the center ring. He had to keep a dozen plates spinning at all times; not one of them could crash to the ground.

But Pastor Nubert didn't mind.

Over the years he had learned to deal with the pressures that came with the ministry. Inevitably his life was surrounded by crises while he was expected to remain calm. Through prayer and discipline, he had discovered one secret to being dependable for those around him: he was organized and punctual beyond reproach. And so although he would rather have sat down and rested for a moment on that cold December evening, he slipped into a jacket and kissed his wife good-bye.

"Be right back," he said. "I need to light the furnace for tonight."

At six-thirty he arrived at West Side Baptist Church on Court Street and LaSalle in the center of the town of Beatrice, Nebraska. The church was something of an anchor, a landmark that everyone in town used when giving directions to outsiders. A stranger could find almost any place in Beatrice as long as he could first find the tall white steeple that marked West Side Baptist Church.

125

Pastor Nubert made his way inside the church building and climbed down two flights of stairs to the basement. There he lit the coal furnace, making sure it was working before he turned to leave. Next he walked up to the sanctuary, where twenty rows of wooden pews made up the seating for Sunday mornings. Glancing at the thermostat, he adjusted it so that the building would be warm in exactly one hour. It was Wednesday. And choir practice was always at seven-thirty on Wednesday evenings.

Glancing once more at his watch, Pastor Nubert quickly left the church and headed home for dinner. He intended to be back at his usual time, no later than seven-fifteen.

*　　　*　　　*

Martha Paul had been the choir director at West Side Baptist Church in Beatrice for sixteen years; as far as she could remember she had never been late to choir practice. Without fail Martha arrived at least fifteen minutes early.

"That way I have time to get the hymnals ready," Martha liked to tell her husband. "I can be sure there are enough sets of choir music, get the lights turned on, and still have time to catch my breath."

Martha had often impressed upon her choir the importance of being on time, reminding them that nothing could be accomplished until every choir member was in his or her place ready to sing.

"A choir is not one or two voices," she would say. "The plan is not to arrive at seven-thirty but to begin singing at seven-thirty."

126

That particularly cold Wednesday evening in December, Martha had every intention of being at church as usual by seven-fifteen. This was to be a special practice since it was the last rehearsal before the church performed its annual Christmas cantata. In addition to the fourteen choir members, there would be a trio of teenage girls joining them. The trio had been working on a musical piece for the cantata, and that night would be the first time the two groups would practice together. More than any other Wednesday it was crucial that she be at church especially early that night.

But she had run into a problem.

Her daughter, Marilyn, had been attending junior college and working part-time to pay tuition. That evening she returned home from her afternoon job and gave a weary nod to her mother.

"I'm going to sleep for a while," she said. "Wake me up for practice."

Marilyn was a pianist and was scheduled to play the piano for the Christmas cantata. Although she had missed choir practice on occasion, her attendance was crucial that evening. So at six-forty-five Martha went upstairs to Marilyn's room and leaned inside.

"Wake up!" she announced. "We're leaving in twenty minutes for practice."

Marilyn moaned and rolled over once in bed. Certain that her daughter was awake and would now get up and get ready for practice, Martha returned to the kitchen.

At seven-ten, when Marilyn had still not emerged from her room, Martha trudged back up the stairs. The young woman lay on her bed still sound asleep.

"Marilyn!" Martha said loudly, moving toward her daughter. "What's wrong with you? You need to wake up right now and get ready. We have to leave!"

Marilyn nodded. "Yeah, I think I'm awake now," she said, shaking her head and opening her eyes wider. "I'll get ready as fast as I can."

Martha went down to wait while her daughter frantically ran around upstairs trying to get ready before her mother had to come up again. But try as she might, she was unable to finish until seven-twenty-five. Just as she came down the stairs toward where her mother stood waiting disapprovingly, the house went pitch-black.

"Great," Martha muttered. "Now we'll really be late."

*   *   *

Donna, Rowena, and Sadie had been best friends since grade school. As far back as they could remember, their families had attended West Side Baptist Church, and for years they had sung in the children's choir. Each of the girls loved to perform, and in their private moments they had always dreamed about forming a singing group and being famous one day after they graduated from high school.

Now that they were teenagers, too old for the youth choir and too young for the senior choir, Martha Paul had devised a way to keep them involved. She created the West Side Girls Trio, a special choir for the three friends in which they could work on musical pieces and perform them occasionally for the congregation.

The number they had been practicing for the Christmas cantata was their most beautiful yet, and none of the girls could wait to present it that evening at practice.

"Let's get there early," Rowena suggested to the others. "That way we can visit a while before practice."

The girls made a plan and arranged for Donna to borrow her father's car and pick up Rowena and Sadie at their homes by seven. That way they could all be at the church by seven-fifteen.

But at seven-ten that evening, after watching out her front window for several seemingly endless minutes, Rowena finally pursed her lips in frustration. Donna was never late when they made plans to do something. She picked up the telephone and dialed her friend's number.

"Hello?" Donna answered.

"Donna? What are you doing? You're supposed to be here to pick me up."

"Rowena, what are you talking about?" Donna said. "I'm waiting for Sadie. I thought she was going to pick both of us up."

"No, that wasn't the plan," Rowena said. "I can't believe this! Now we're all going to be late and no one's going to take us seriously."

"Ro, I'm telling you Sadie is supposed to be doing the driving tonight."

Rowena sighed. She had no transportation other than catching rides from her friends, and she was determined to work out their misunderstandings so that they could get to choir practice.

At seven-twenty-five Donna called and explained that she had the car keys in her hand, Sadie was waiting outside, and she was on her way out the door. Just before the girls hung up, everything in both their houses went black.

Theodore Charles was not accustomed to being apart from his wife, Anne. The couple had been married fifteen years and had rarely spent a day away from each other during that time. But that spring Anne had some family matters to attend to in nearby Lincoln, and she wouldn't be home until the next morning.

"Don't worry, Theodore," she told him before she left. "I've made plans for you and the boys. You'll be hav-

129

ing supper with the McKinters on Wednesday night while I'm in Lincoln."

Theodore was pleased with this arrangement. The McKinters were a kind couple well past retirement age, and Margaret McKinter was one of the best cooks in Beatrice. He knew that he and the boys, ages eight and ten, would be in good hands while Anne was gone.

They even had plans for after the meal. Wednesday night was choir practice, and he and Anne usually took the boys along with them. The fact that Anne was gone didn't change things. Theodore and the boys would have dinner at the McKinters' at six o'clock and leave shortly after seven so they would make practice early enough to visit with his friend, Herb Kipf, since both men were busy the rest of the week and rarely had time to talk.

As he'd expected, Margaret McKinter's meal was wonderful: corned beef with biscuits and gravy and homemade apple pie for dessert.

"I must say, Margaret," Theodore commented after the meal. "You make the meanest apple pie this side of the Blue River."

"Oh, now, that ain't so," Margaret gushed. "That pretty little wife of yours makes a pie just as fine as any around town. I remember when she was just a wee little thing, that Annie girl. Yes, sir, just a little girl with the prettiest dresses and . . ."

Theodore had expected this. Along with Margaret's good cooking, she was also quite the conversationalist. Often a person could rest ten or fifteen minutes while

Margaret did a fine job of carrying on a conversation all by herself.

That being the case, Theodore was not surprised to find himself nodding in agreement and glancing at his watch as seven-fifteen slipped past. At seven-twenty-five he silently determined to cut into Margaret's monologue, apologize profusely, and quickly exit with his boys before he missed choir practice altogether.

"And so like I was saying"—Margaret McKinter drew in a quick breath—"whenever Thelma does her laundry without the bleach—I'm talking about her underclothes and all the rest—and then hangs them out to dry on the—"

Suddenly everything in the McKinter house went dark, and for the first time in nearly an hour there was utter silence in the room.

Gina Hicks was unsure about what to do that evening. She very much enjoyed being a member of the West Side Baptist Church choir and planned on singing a solo in the upcoming Christmas cantata. Certainly the choir director would expect her at practice since the performance was less than two weeks away.

But then there was her mother to consider.

Norma Hicks was a charter member of the Ladies' Missionary Group, which met one Thursday each month at a different home. That month the women planned to meet at the Hickses' home, and the meeting was set for the following night.

"Gina, I know you need to go to practice," her mother had said earlier in the evening. "But I could really use your help. Besides cleaning, I have some baking to do, and I'd like to get it all finished tonight."

Gina's younger sisters and brother would be taking their baths and getting ready for bed, and Gina knew there was no one else to help her mother. Still, she struggled with her decision. She lived so close to the church she could hurry right home after practice to help her mother. But maybe her mother really needed her, and in that case she would definitely stay home.

Gina looked at the clock. Seven-twenty. There was still time to get to the church before practice. She'd just begun searching for her coat when she heard her mother struggling to break up an argument between her two sisters.

132

Gina sighed softly.

"Mom!" she yelled across the house. "Don't worry about things. I'll stay and help."

After all, she figured, God might want her to sing in the choir—but first he'd want her to help her mother. She began humming the melody to her solo number and headed toward the kitchen. Quickly she dialed her friend and fellow choir member, Agnes O'Shaugnessy.

"I won't be there tonight. Tell Mrs. Paul I'm working on my number, and I'll get with her about it later."

"Okay, Mary and I are just about to leave. We'll let her know."

Gina hung up the phone, but just as she began washing dishes, there was a distant roar. Suddenly the windows began rattling and the ground beneath her feet began to shake.

Norma came flying down the stairs with the younger girls racing behind her. "Oh, dear Lord!" she cried out. "What in heaven's name was that?"

At that instant they were enveloped in black.

Mary Jones and Agnes O'Shaugnessy were young mothers who always carpooled to choir practice at West Side Baptist Church. Usually by seven o'clock they had finished dinner and gotten their toddler-aged children ready for bed so that their husbands would have no trouble taking over while they attended practice.

That Wednesday it was Mary's turn to drive, and she arrived at Agnes's house at seven-fifteen. Agnes lived just two blocks from the church, so usually the two women talked for a few minutes before leaving for practice. But on that night Agnes was caught up in the final segment of a favorite TV show and she motioned for Mary to sit down.

"This is great," she said. "You've got to see this guy."

The program was one of the neighborhood favorites, and Mary soon found herself hooked. Even after the phone call from Gina Hicks, Mary and Agnes continued to watch the program. Before either woman realized what had happened, it was seven-twenty-five.

"Oh, no!" Agnes gasped. "We're going to be late. I'm so sorry, Mary. I lost all track of time."

Mary stood up quickly, eyes still turned to the final

moments of the television show. Just then Agnes's husband, Paul, joined them with the baby in his arms.

"Aren't you going to be late, girls?" he asked, looking at the clock.

"Nah," Mary said. "Besides, I love this show, and we'll still be there by seven-thirty. The church is just around the corner."

In less than a minute the credits began rolling on the screen as the program ended, and both women said good-bye to Paul and headed for the car. Just as they opened the car door, they heard the sound of a terrifying explosion, the force of which shook the ground and nearly knocked them off their feet.

134

Pastor Nubert had finished dinner by seven o'clock that evening and was helping his wife with the dishes. Susan, their six-year-old daughter, was already dressed and waiting by the front door, so their evening was right on schedule. The pastor smiled. He was looking forward to choir practice since the cantata was coming up so quickly. Everyone was excited about the performance, and it brought an even greater purpose to their gathering together and singing.

"Should be a good turnout tonight," he commented to his wife.

Before she could answer, Susan walked into the kitchen.

"Daddy, I'm thirsty," she complained.

Pastor Nubert looked at the clock on the wall. Seven-oh-five. They needed to leave in the next two minutes if they wanted to arrive by seven-fifteen.

"Honey, can't you wait until after practice? We'll have punch and cookies when we're all done singing," he said, stooping to her level and brushing a lock of hair from her eyes.

The little girl shook her head adamantly. "My throat hurts and I want a drink now, please," she said politely. "Please, Daddy."

The pastor sighed. "All right, but we have to leave in just a minute. Drink it quickly, okay?"

Susan clapped her hands happily. "Yes, Daddy. I will."

He walked to the refrigerator and pulled out a pitcher of red punch, then poured some into a cup and handed it to her.

"Thanks, Daddy," she said, turning around and walking out of the kitchen. Pastor Nubert watched as the child rounded the corner into the living room and then tripped on the throw rug, dumping the red drink down her pinafore dress. Immediately the liquid seeped into the beige rug, and Susan cried for help.

"I'm so sorry, Daddy. I didn't mean to." Tears had formed in her eyes, and the pastor's heart went out to her. He moved quickly to the little girl's side. "It's okay, sweetie. We'll clean it up."

In an instant, the child's mother joined them with a rag and a bucket of water, working as fast as she could to dilute the stain on the carpet and clean off Susan's dress.

"You'll need to change, dear," she said patiently.

The pastor looked at the clock once more. Seven-thirteen.

"We're going to be late," he muttered as their daughter left the room.

"Everybody should be late once in his life," his wife said with a smile. "Don't let it kill you, George."

He sighed again and began helping with the cleanup. "You're right. Go help Susan. We'll get there when we get there."

Fourteen minutes later, just as the Nuberts had finished cleaning up the mess and were preparing to leave for practice, the house suddenly shuddered and the lights went out. They were left standing in utter darkness.

"What is it, George?" his wife whispered. "What do you think happened?"

The pastor held his car keys in his hand and led his family carefully through the unlit house to the front door. "I don't know. Let's get down to the church and see if the lights are off there, too."

Herb Kipf had finished dinner and was working on a letter he was writing to the secretary of another Baptist church across town. He often helped out with paperwork in the church office and that included writing letters.

At age twenty-nine, Herb was a machinist and a bachelor who lived at home with his parents. He often worked long hours and nearly every day volunteered some of this time down at West Side Baptist Church. He'd been a member of the congregation all his life, and he'd sung in the choir since he was twelve. In fact, most of the choir was made up of a core of people who had sung together for the past seventeen years. "Herb, aren't you going to be late for choir?" his mother called to him that evening. "It's ten after seven."

Herb glanced at the clock in his bedroom and was surprised to see that the time had slipped by so quickly. He had planned to be at practice by seven-fifteen so he could visit with Theodore Charles and his other friends. But now he'd be doing well to get there by seven-thirty. He wrote more quickly, and by seven-twenty-five he sealed the envelope, stamped it, and stood up to leave.

Racing down the stairs of his parents' home, Herb shouted good-bye to his family and ran outside to his car. But just before he drove away, his mother burst through the front door and motioned for him to roll down his car window.

137

"What is it, Mom? I'm in a hurry," he yelled.

She jogged to the car, and Herb could see that she looked deeply distressed. "Herb," she said breathlessly. "Gladys just called and it's the church. It blew up! Just a minute ago, at seven-twenty-seven."

Herb's face fell and his stomach turned over. If the church had blown up at seven-twenty-seven, it could mean only one thing. Many of his closest friends had been inside. He nodded to his mother and headed for the church, praying as he drove that at least some members of the West Side Baptist Church choir had somehow survived the explosion.

As he approached the church, Herb could see numerous fire trucks and police officers and dozens of people gathering on the sidewalk to see what had happened. He stared at where the church should have been and was horrified. The building had been leveled and was nothing but a smoldering pile of splintered wood and crumbled bricks. He moved his car slowly around the emergency vehicles and saw the towering white steeple. The twenty-foot-high section of the building had been severed from the church in the explosion and now lay exactly where he and the other singers usually parked their cars.

"Dear God, who was inside?" Herb whispered in horror as he made his way quickly from his car to the fire chief.

138

"Ernie!" Herb called frantically. He could hear people screaming and crying as they stared at the flattened church, and he tried not to imagine how many of his friends had been inside the building when it exploded. Sirens wailed through the night, and the air was filled with heavy smoke and settling debris. It had been dark for a couple of hours, and it was difficult to see clearly.

"Thank God," the fire chief said as he made his way to Herb and put a hand on his shoulder. "I thought you must have been inside. Don't you have choir practice tonight?"

Tears filled Herb's eyes as he nodded. "Yes, I was late. But the others . . . Ernie, they must be inside. It's after seven-thirty. What happened?"

"The whole thing just blew up. Probably a natural gas leak. The steeple sliced through the power lines, knocked out power all over town. Windows are blown out, too. Up and down the block." Ernie bowed his head a moment. "I hate to tell you this, but if anyone was inside they didn't have a chance."

"Have they looked?" Herb strained to see the area where the church had stood. "Someone might need help."

Ernie shook his head. "They've given a quick check, Herb. There wouldn't be any bodies to identify. It looks like a bomb went off. And anything in the basement is buried under tons of rubble."

The fire chief looked intently at his friend, not sure if he was up to the task he was about to give him.

"Herb, there's a lot of frantic people standing around, and they need some answers. Please, walk around and gather all the choir members you can find. We need to know who's missing."

It was the most frightening task Herb had ever attempted. He took a deep breath and headed toward the church looking desperately into the night for the faces of choir members among the crowd. Debris cluttered the area and Herb had to step over piles of shattered church pews and roof tiles as he began to search.

Just then he saw the three teenagers who had planned to join them that night, Donna, Rowena, and Sadie. He was filled with relief as he reached them and pulled them into a group hug.

"Thank God," he said.

Donna was crying too hard to talk, and Rowena seemed stunned. "We got mixed up about who was driving," she said, staring at the flattened church. "We were ten minutes late. Just ten minutes!"

Herb pointed the girls toward the fire chief and told them they needed to wait there. "We have to find out who was inside," he said.

At that Rowena began to sob.

"Rowena, keep hold of yourself," Herb said. There was no time for hysterics, not with so many people still unaccounted for.

"Pray, Rowena," he said. "Just pray."

The girls followed Herb's orders, and he continued through the crowd, which was growing constantly. Just then he saw Theodore Charles with his two young sons huddled next to him. The men were such good friends that Herb began crying unashamedly in relief.

140

"Theodore!" Herb yelled. "Over here!"

Theodore spotted Herb and with his sons in tow walked quickly to meet him. "We were late," Theodore said. "Mrs. McKinter talked too long." He looked at his friend intently. "Otherwise we'd be dead."

"I was late, too," Herb said. "Writing a letter; time just got away from me." He paused a moment. For the first time he considered the truth. He should have been inside the church when it exploded. Every other Wednesday night as far back as he could remember, he had arrived at choir practice fifteen minutes early. He hugged his friend tightly and sent him toward the fire chief.

For fifteen minutes Herb maneuvered frantically through the crowd. He found Pastor Nubert, his wife, and their daughter, Susan. There were quick hugs exchanged, and Herb pointed them toward the fire captain with the others. A few minutes later he found Mary Jones and Agnes O'Shaugnessy, and three retired women, each of whom had come separately and who had a different reason for being late to practice that evening. Soon afterward he found a young couple who had only joined the choir the year before. They had received a long-distance phone call, which had made them late that evening.

Finally Herb came upon the choir director, Martha, and her daughter, Marilyn.

"Martha!" Herb hugged the crying woman and let her rest on his shoulder for a moment. "I thought for sure you'd be inside."

"Marilyn couldn't wake up," she sobbed. "I tried and tried to get her up, but she just kept sleeping." She looked up at Herb, her eyes red and her face tear-stained. "Do you know that in sixteen years I've never been here later than seven-twenty?" she asked, her eyes filled with awe.

141

"The church blew at seven-twenty-seven," Herb said gravely, pointing Martha and Marilyn toward the others. "Let's go join the others. We need to know who's still missing."

Herb felt as though he were in the middle of a strange and twisted dream. First there was the horror of seeing the church leveled by an explosion, and then the miracles, one after another, of finding each choir member alive. How was it possible that so many people had been late for so many different reasons?

There were fourteen choir members, three teenage singers, and three children who should have been at choir that night. After a quick count, Herb was stunned to learn that only one person was missing.

"Gina Hicks?" he yelled so that the other choir members could hear him. "Anyone seen Gina?"

"She couldn't come tonight," Agnes said happily, wiping tears from her eyes. "She called and said she had to help her mother."

That made twenty people. Every choir member was accounted for.

Just then Erma Rimrock, a retired woman who had been a member of the church for forty years, approached the huddled choir.

142

"Thank God, you're all alive," she said. Then she turned to Pastor Nubert. "Pastor, last week my brother and I purchased the old closed-down Methodist church down the street as an investment. I want you to know you can hold services there as long as you need to. The Christmas cantata will work out just fine there. We'll all be here tomorrow to salvage what we can from the mess. And with a little cleaning at the other building we should be able to meet this Sunday."

The pastor was stunned. There was no explanation for anything that had happened that night, including Erma's offer. He hugged her and thanked her, and then turned back to Herb.

"We're all accounted for?" he asked, still amazed.

Herb nodded and looked at the faces in front of him, each struggling with the nearness of disaster as they stood silent and shivering in the freezing winter night. For nearly a minute no one said a word as they realized the certainty of the miracle they had been a part of.

"I think we should join hands," Herb said softly. The choir separated itself from the milling crowd and found a spot in the middle of Court Street where they formed a circle.

"Do you understand this?" he asked them. "Every one of us was late tonight. Every single one of us."

"Let's pray," Pastor Nubert suggested, and instantly everyone in the circle bowed their heads.

"Dear Lord—" The pastor's voice cracked with emotion and he struggled to continue. "Lord, we know that you saved us tonight from certain death. By delaying each of us ten minutes, you have proved yourself beyond a doubt, and we thank you."

The pastor squeezed the hands of his wife and daughter and looked at the other faces around him. Then looking upward, he spoke in a voice that was barely audible. "Thank you, God. We will not forget this."

Then, with the townspeople looking on, the West Side Baptist Choir held hands and sang "Silent Night" in a performance Beatrice, Nebraska, remembers to this day.

About the Author

KAREN KINGSBURY is America's favorite inspirational storyteller. She is the author of ten #1 bestselling books and more than thirty other emotionally gripping novels, several of which have been adapted for film and television. Previously a staff writer for the *Los Angeles Times* and a *People* magazine contributor, Karen lives with her husband and six children in the Pacific Northwest.

Reading Group Guide

1. Do you believe in miracles? Why or why not?

2. Have you seen God work a miracle in your life or the life of someone you know? Explain.

3. Why are we more inclined to look for miracles at Christmastime? Do you think there really is something different about this time of year? Explain.

4. In the story "That Silent Night," a plane is guided into an airstrip by a voice coming from a closed airport. Tell about a time when you or someone you know experienced an impossible rescue.

5. In the story "A Helping Hand," people pulled together to give financial assistance to a stranger. Tell about a time when you or someone you know experienced financial assistance or aided in financial assistance at Christmastime.

6. In "The Most Wonderful Time of the Year," a woman asks if God will take her home to heaven instead of taking the young father in the hospital room down the hall. What are your thoughts on this situation? Have you seen God answer an unusual prayer request for you or someone you know? Explain.

7. The story "Jessica's Gift" tells of the miracle of reconciliation. Have you seen God work this type of miracle in your life or the life of someone you know? Explain.

8. "A Touch of Heaven" discusses the story of a physical healing. Describe a time when you or someone you know experienced a physical healing after praying about the problem.

9. Why do you think that sometimes God answers our prayers for healing with a miracle and other times a person remains physically ill or even dies? Does this affect the way you look at God or prayer? Explain.

10. In the story "Home for Christmas," a family is given a very unusual miracle—one of reassurance. Discuss a time when you or someone you know experienced a miracle like this one.

11. "A Gift for Noel" tells about a deaf little girl and her miracle gift of a deaf kitten. Some people might call this a coincidence. Tell about a time when you or someone you know experienced something miraculous that others might think was a coincidence. Share your thoughts.

12. The story "The First Day of Christmas" tells about God's amazing rescue by way of something that was clearly impossible. Do you believe impossible things can happen as God's way of protecting us? Explain.

13. The story "Unexpected Christmas Package" tells about the discovery of a precious ring, one that had been missing for more than a decade. Do you think God cares

about our prayers for things that the world might not see as significant? Give an example of a time when you or someone you know experienced a dramatic answer or even a miracle when what was at stake might not have mattered to anyone else.

14. "Christmas Angels" is the story of a lost little boy and the mysterious women who helped him find his way back to his mother. Hebrews 13 tells us that we must be careful to entertain strangers, for, in doing so, some have entertained angels without knowing it. Do you think the women in this story were angels? Why or why not?

15. Do you believe in angels? Tell about a time when you or someone you know experienced a strange encounter with someone who might've been an angel.

16. "The Holy Hand of God" presents a miraculous situation where a car accident was averted in a way that was unexplainable. Has this sort of thing ever happened to you or someone you know? Explain.

17. In "His Mysterious Ways," God reunited two people who had been neighbors as children, in a very dramatic and instrumental manner. Have you ever reconnected with someone and found the results to be dramatic? Explain. Could this be a miracle?

18. "Christmas Roses" tells about a comforting smell that came without any apparent reason. Do you believe God would provide such a thing to bring comfort to one of his children? Why or why not?

19. The story of "Heavenly Hindrances" is almost unbelievable. God orchestrated it so that not one of the people who should've been there was in the church building when it exploded. Tell about a time when you or someone you know was delayed and, because of the delay, their life was saved. Do you think this is a coincidence or a miracle? Explain.

20. Talk about the ways these true stories have touched and grown your faith. What Christmas miracle are you praying for right now? Share it. Commit to pray for your friends and loved ones throughout the season.